THE DEMAND FOR LIQUID ASSETS:
A TEMPORAL CROSS-SECTION ANALYSIS

1963 Award Winner

THE FORD FOUNDATION DOCTORAL
DISSERTATION SERIES

THE DEMAND FOR LIQUID ASSETS:

A TEMPORAL CROSS-SECTION ANALYSIS

EDGAR L. FEIGE

*Assistant Professor
of Economics
The University of Wisconsin*

PRENTICE - HALL , INC .

Englewood Cliffs, N. J.

To my parents, with gratitude

1960 Award Winners

Bernard H. Baum *Decentralization of Authority in a Bureaucracy*
  Dissertation submitted to Department of Sociology, University of Chicago

Leon V. Hirsch *Marketing in an Underdeveloped Economy: The North Indian Sugar Industry*
  Dissertation submitted to Graduate School of Business Administration, Harvard University

Bedros Peter Pashigian *The Distribution of Automobiles, an Economic Analysis of the Franchise System*
  Dissertation submitted to Department of Economics, Massachusetts Institute of Technology

Martin Patchen *The Choice of Wage Comparison*
  Dissertation submitted to Department of Social Psychology, University of Michigan

Fred M. Tonge *A Heuristic Program for Assembly Line Balancing*
  Dissertation submitted to Graduate School of Industrial Administration, Carnegie Institute of Technology

1959 Award Winners

Kalman J. Cohen *Computer Models of the Shoe, Leather, Hide Sequence*
  Dissertation submitted to Graduate School of Industrial Administration, Carnegie Institute of Technology

Bob R. Holdren *The Structure of a Retail Market and the Market Behavior of Retail Units*
  Dissertation submitted to Department of Economics, Yale University

Frank Proschan *Polya Type Distributions in Renewal Theory, with an Application to an Inventory Problem*
  Dissertation submitted to Department of Statistics, Stanford University

Andrew C. Stedry *Budget Control and Cost Behavior*
  Dissertation submitted to Graduate School of Industrial Administration, Carnegie Institute of Technology

Victor H. Vroom *Some Personality Determinants of the Effects of Participation*
  Dissertation submitted to Department of Psychology, University of Michigan

1962 Award Winners

Alexander Barges *The Effect of Capital Structure on the Cost of Capital*
Dissertation submitted to Graduate School of Business Administration, Northwestern University

Charles P. Bonini *Simulation of Information and Decision Systems in the Firm*
Dissertation submitted to Graduate School of Business, Carnegie Institute of Technology

James M. Ferguson *The Advertising Rate Structure in the Daily Newspaper Industry*
Dissertation submitted to Department of Economics, University of Chicago

Gordon M. Kaufman *Statistical Decision and Related Techniques in Oil and Gas Exploration*
Dissertation submitted to Graduate School of Business, Harvard University

H. Martin Weingartner *Mathematical Programming and the Analysis of Capital Budgeting Problems*
Dissertation submitted to Graduate School of Industrial Administration Carnegie Institute of Technology

1961 Award Winners

Geoffrey P. E. Clarkson *Portfolio Selection: A Simulation of Trust Investment*
Dissertation submitted to Graduate School of Industrial Administration, Carnegie Institute of Technology

Donald E. Farrar *The Investment Decision Under Uncertainty: Portfolio Selection*
Dissertation submitted to Faculty of Arts and Sciences, Harvard University

Richard S. Hatch *An Evaluation of a Forced-Choice Differential Accuracy Approach to the Measurement of Supervisory Empathy*
Dissertation submitted to Department of Psychology, University of Minnesota

David Meiselman *The Term Structure of Interest Rates*
Dissertation submitted to Department of Economics, University of Chicago

George William Summers *Financing and Initial Operations of New Firms*
Dissertation submitted to Department of Management, Case Institute of Technology

Foreword

Dr. Feige's dissertation, completed during the academic year 1962–1963, is one of six selected for publication in the fifth annual Doctoral Dissertation Competition sponsored by the Program in Economic Development and Administration of the Ford Foundation.

The intent of the doctoral dissertation competition has been to recognize and encourage excellence in research on business by graduate students. Publication awards, now totaling twenty-six, have been made over the five years of the competition to persons granted doctorates in business and related fields whose thesis research on problems of business was especially distinguished by its analytical content and strong roots in the underlying disciplines common to business.

In addition to Dr. Feige's, the dissertations published this year are:

An Evaluation of Level of Aspiration As a Training Procedure
        Forrest W. Fryer
        Department of Psychology
        University of Maryland

The Demand for Physical Capital: Application of a Wealth Model
        Frederick S. Hammer
        Graduate School of Industrial Administration
        Carnegie Institute of Technology

The Measurement of Cumulative Advertising Effects
        Kristian S. Palda
        Graduate School of Business
        University of Chicago

Some Large-Scale Production Scheduling Problems in the Paper Industry
        John F. Pierce, Jr.
        School of Industrial Management
        Massachusetts Institute of Technology

*The Economics of Discretionary Behavior: Managerial Objectives in a
Theory of the Firm*
> Oliver E. Williamson
> Graduate School of Industrial Administration
> Carnegie Institute of Technology

On behalf of the Ford Foundation, I wish to express my gratitude to the members of the Editorial Committee for the care and thought they devoted to the selection process. The members of this Committee, who made the final selection of winning dissertations, were: Professor Robert Ferber of the University of Illinois, Professor Mason Haire of the University of California at Berkeley, and Professor Thomas L. Whisler of the University of Chicago.

The Editorial Committee's task was considerably lightened by the assistance of twelve readers, experts in the wide range of disciplines covered in the competition, who carefully screened the theses submitted. The Foundation joins the Committee in acknowledging their debt to Professors Paul E. Breer of Cornell University, Earl F. Cheit and Lyman W. Porter of the University of California at Berkeley, James R. Jackson of the University of California at Los Angeles, Arch R. Dooley of Harvard University, Daniel M. Holland of the Massachusetts Institute of Technology, Robert J. Holloway of the University of Minnesota, Donald P. Jacobs of Northwestern University, Bernard Karsh of the University of Illinois, Walter G. Kell of the University of Michigan, E. W. Martin, Jr. of Indiana University, and Joseph W. Newman of Stanford University.

With the publication of these latest winners, the Doctoral Dissertation Competition has completed its planned five-year span. My colleagues and I wish to express our appreciation for the generous assistance which the Ford Foundation has received from many people: Faculty members too numerous to mention have read and screened the more than 250 dissertations which have been submitted during the life of the competition, and Prentice-Hall has contributed its services to the publicizing and publishing of the selected dissertations.

> CLARENCE H. FAUST
> VICE PRESIDENT
> THE FORD FOUNDATION

New York, N.Y.
January, 1964

Acknowledgments

The research which formed the basis of this study was supported by a fellowship grant from the Federal Reserve Bank of Chicago. Additional support for the study was granted by the Workshop in Money and Banking (University of Chicago) and the Social Systems Research Institute (University of Wisconsin).

I am especially indebted to Professor Milton Friedman for his generous aid and encouragement during the early stages of the study. I also received helpful comments from the other members of my dissertation committee, Professors Martin Bailey, Robert Basmann, and Harry Johnson.

The continual encouragement and support received from my colleagues at the University of Wisconsin made possible the completion of the study.

Mrs. Anna Campbell cheerfully and accurately typed several drafts of the study. Thanks are also due Mrs. Alice Wilcox who typed the tables.

EDGAR L. FEIGE

Contents

xi

Contents

Introduction

Economists have long been divided about the role of the quantity of money in determining such target variables as the level of income and prices. Although much of the controversy has been couched in theoretical terms, the substantive issues which divide economists are primarily empirical rather than theoretical. The purpose of this study is to clarify some of these empirical issues, particularly as they relate to the effectiveness of monetary policy in a world of complex financial intermediation.

Chapter 1 considers the empirical problems of selecting a specific subset of assets which corresponds most closely with the theoretical concept of *money* referred to in both Keynesian and neo-classical models of income and price determination. Chapter 2 reviews the mechanism by which monetary policy affects such target variables as the level of income and prices in a regime of financial intermediation and financial innovation. Emphasis is placed on isolating the substantive empirical issues relevant to recent controversies about the effectiveness of monetary policy. The following empirical hypotheses are most relevant to the effectiveness of monetary policy:

1. The liabilities of non-bank financial intermediaries are close substitutes for money (defined as some subset of those assets whose supply is regulated by the monetary authorities).

2. The demand for money is a stable function of a limited number of variables.

3. The demand for money is independent of the supply of money.

The foregoing hypotheses are examined in Chapter 3 by estimating demand functions for demand deposits, for time deposits in commercial banks and savings and loan association shares, and by testing the magnitude and stability of the parameters of the estimated functions.

1

Temporal cross-section data are utilized, and the demand functions are estimated by means of single equation least squares and restricted efficient estimation procedures.

The results of the empirical tests and the implications of the results for monetary policy are elaborated in the concluding chapter.

CHAPTER 1

The Definition of Money

The problem of constructing an appropriate definition of money has plagued economists since the middle of the nineteenth century, when it blossomed into the famous currency–banking school controversy. This controversy was stimulated by the rapid industrial and financial changes in the English economy. The growth of note-issuing stock banks and the growing relative importance of bank deposits motivated economists to consider the effects of these institutional changes on the stability of the monetary mechanism. The question whether the definition of money should be broadened to include the deposit liabilities of the banking system became a focal point of the historic discussion.

In recent years, Raymond Goldsmith's study of financial intermediaries awakened economists' interest in investigating the effects of these rapidly growing intermediaries on the monetary mechanism.[1] Once again, the question arose whether the liabilities of these financial intermediaries should be included in the definition of money. Unfortunately, most theoretical literature side-stepped the explicit problem of defining money, so that the empirical worker was left with the problem of choosing among alternative definitions. The use of different definitions of money in various empirical studies of the demand for money has contributed greatly to the difficulty of arriving at some consistent conclusions concerning the parameters and the stability of the demand for money.

---

[1] Raymond W. Goldsmith, *Financial Intermediaries in the American Economy Since 1900* (Princeton: Princeton University Press, 1958).

Harry Johnson, in his survey of monetary theory and policy, distinguishes four main schools of thought concerning the definition of money.[1] The most common definition adopted in empirical studies classifies currency and demand deposits as money. This definition is often rationalized on the ground that these are the only two assets which function directly as a medium of exchange. This classification, based on a particular functional characteristic of monetary assets, was employed by Latané, who justified the narrow definition because it avoids all the complexities of the near monies which are not a final means of payment.[2]

Another group of empirical workers has rejected the preceding classification scheme. Milton Friedman and David Meiselman have argued that there are no legitimate a priori grounds upon which to base a definition of money; instead, an empirical criterion should be established which is capable of discriminating among alternative definitions.[3] Operationally, Friedman and Meiselman chose that particular definition of money which "put the theory in its best light." Having experimented with various subsets of assets, Friedman and Meiselman chose currency, demand deposits, and time deposits in commercial banks as their definition of money. In repeated experiments, this particular magnitude displayed a closer relationship to income than did alternative formulations and was therefore adopted in their study. They argue that "the appropriate reason for including time deposits is not simply that they are highly correlated with income, but that they are such close substitutes for other monetary items that it is preferable to treat them as if they were *perfect substitutes* than to omit them."

Although this may be a useful criterion for defining money in a highly simplified model of income determination, Friedman goes on to utilize the broader definition in estimating the demand function for money.[4] Friedman justifies the inclusion of time deposits pragmatically

---

[1] Harry G. Johnson, "Monetary Theory and Policy," *American Economic Review*, **LII** (June, 1962), 335–84.

[2] H. A. Latané, "Cash Balances and the Interest Rate—A Pragmatic Approach," *Review of Economics and Statistics*, **XXXVI** (November, 1954), 456–60; also "Income Velocity and Interest Rates: A Pragmatic Approach," *Review of Economics and Statistics*, **XLII** (November, 1960), 445–49.

[3] Milton Friedman and David Meiselman, "The Relative Stability of Monetary Velocity and the Investment Multiplier in the United States, 1897–1958." (Forthcoming publication of the Commission on Money and Credit.)

[4] Milton Friedman, "The Demand for Money: Some Theoretical and Empirical Results," National Bureau of Economic Research, *Occasional Paper* 68, 1959.

on the ground that separate estimates of demand and of time deposits are not available before 1914. The inclusion of time deposits in the definition of money, however, confounds the effects of "the rate of interest" on the demand for money. The rate of interest is usually regarded as a measure of the opportunity cost of holding non-interest–earning cash balances, and thus a rise in the rate of interest is expected to cause a reduction in the demand for money as narrowly defined. When time deposits are included in the definition of money, the rate of interest plays a dual role. On the one hand, the rate of interest represents the opportunity cost of holding currency and demand deposits; on the other hand, the interest rate can be viewed as a proxy variable for the yield on time deposits. Since the two effects on the demand for money (broadly defined) are in opposite directions, it is not surprising that the rate of interest does a poor job of explaining variations in the demand for money in Friedman's study.

Instead of treating demand deposits and time deposits as if they were *perfect substitutes*, an alternative to the Friedman-Meiselman aggregation scheme is to estimate separate demand functions for demand deposits and time deposits. Each demand function would include as arguments the rates of return on assets which are believed to be close substitutes for the asset in question. This method would be preferable to the Friedman-Meiselman approach since it avoids the extreme assumption of perfect substitutability and allows an explicit determination of the true substitution relationships.

John Gurley similarly rejected the notion that assets could be analytically classified on a priori grounds.[1] Recognizing the possibility that all liabilities of financial institutions could be classified as money, Gurley suggested a definition of money comprised of a weighted sum of a host of financial liabilities; the particular weights were chosen such that the weighted sum, as a ratio of income, would bear a close relationship to movements in short- and long-term interest rates. For illustrative purposes, Gurley selected a definition which assigned weights of one to currency and demand deposits, and weights of one-half to time deposits, savings and loan association shares, mutual savings bank deposits, credit union shares, postal savings deposits, policy reserves on life insurance, and U.S. savings bonds. His own calculations suggest, however, that a narrow definition of money worked equally

---

[1] John G. Gurley, *Liquidity and Financial Institutions in the Postwar Economy.* Study Paper 14, Joint Economic Committee, 86th Cong., 2nd Sess., Washington, 1960.

well in explaining interest rate movements in the postwar period. Although Gurley made no attempt to derive "the best" set of weights, such weights could be obtained by the use of canonical correlation techniques.

Gurley's most significant contribution to the discussion was his explicit recognition that any definition of money must ultimately take account of the substitution relationships between a variety of assets and money, as narrowly defined. Although these substitution relationships are not examined explicitly, Gurley suggests that the weights given to different assets have a direct relationship to the degree of substitution among assets. Thus an implicit weight of zero, given to a particular asset, implies that this asset and money, as narrowly defined, are independent in demand, whereas a weight of unity implies that the two assets are perfect substitutes. Gurley's own belief that liabilities of financial intermediaries are imperfect substitutes for money leads him to select weights whose magnitude is between zero and one.

Gurley proposes that the ratio of a weighted sum of liquid assets to income depends upon "the rate of interest" such that

$$(1.1) \qquad \frac{\sum_{i=1}^{n} \alpha_i z_i}{Y} = f(r),$$

where $z_1, \ldots, z_n$ represent the liabilities of financial intermediaries and currency; $\alpha_1, \ldots, \alpha_n$ represent an arbitrary set of weights; Y, income; and r, "the rate of interest." Assuming that the relationship is linear, we may write

$$(1.2) \qquad \frac{\sum_{i=1}^{n} \alpha_i z_i}{Y} = a + br.$$

Now "the rate of interest" can be regarded as a weighted average of all interest rates; therefore, Eq. (1.2) can be rewritten as

$$(1.3) \qquad \frac{\sum_{i=1}^{n} \alpha_i z_i}{Y} = a + b \sum_{k=1}^{n} w_k r_k,$$

implying a demand function for the ith asset of

$$(1.4) \qquad z_i = \frac{1}{\alpha_i} \left[Ya + Yb \sum_{k=1}^{n} w_k r_k - \sum_{k \neq i}^{n} \alpha_k z_k \right].$$

Substitutability between any two assets is traditionally defined by the sign and the magnitude of the partial derivative of quantity with respect to price, holding utility constant. Assuming that the indirect income effect of a change in price is negligible, we can partially differentiate (1.4) with respect to a particular rate of return in order to derive the direct substitution effect as a function of the asset weights.

$$(1.5) \qquad \frac{\partial z_i}{\partial r_j} = \frac{1}{\alpha_i} \left[Ybw_j - \sum_{k \neq i}^{n} \alpha_k \frac{\partial z_k}{\partial r_j} \right].$$

When z_i is money, as narrowly defined, then, according to Gurley, $\alpha_i = 1$, and α_j should represent the degree of substitutability between z_i and z_j, which is traditionally measured by $\partial z_i / \partial r_j$. However,

$$(1.6) \qquad \alpha_j = \frac{Ybw_j - \sum_{k \neq j}^{n} \alpha_k \, \partial z_k / \partial r_j}{\partial z_j / \partial r_j} \, ;$$

i.e., each weight depends not only on the corresponding substitution term, but also on the non-corresponding substitution terms.

The preceding demonstration does not imply that substitution relationships are irrelevant in specifying the demand for money, but rather that Gurley's method of specification is erroneous. Recognizing that the liabilities of financial intermediaries may be close substitutes for money does not imply that money should be defined to include these liabilities but, simply, that the demand function for money—defined to correspond to some quantity which the monetary authorities can regulate—must include as arguments the explicit rates of return on these alternative forms of holding wealth.

An alternative method of defining money has been proposed by the authors of the Radcliff Report. These economists regard *liquidity* as the relevant monetary magnitude but have never offered an explicit operational definition of the term. As Johnson points out, "this school ... does not so much advance a theory as assert a position"; and in the absence of a theory of the relationship between *liquidity* and target variables, this position contributes little toward clarifying the problem of choosing an appropriate monetary magnitude.

The preceding alternative methods of defining money have contributed to the general confusion regarding the behavior of the demand for money. Richard Selden, in his study of monetary velocity in the United States, recognized that many of the apparent conflicts concerning the behavior of the demand for money would "vanish if a common definition of money had been employed."[1] The main issue regarding the definition has clearly been whether or not to include assets which seem to be relatively close substitutes for money, as it is narrowly defined. Analytically, it seems preferable to define money as some subset of assets which the monetary authorities can influence and to introduce money substitutes into the analysis as factors affecting the demand for money. In particular, changes in the rates of return on money substitutes will affect the demand for money as narrowly defined. Including such rates explicitly in the analysis is preferable to defining money more broadly, since the former approach avoids arbitrary assumptions concerning the degree of substitutability and allows the empirical evidence to specify the exact nature of the substitution relationships. This approach introduces the empirical problem of trying to isolate the effects of particular interest rates when all rates may be highly collinear in time series analyses. This latter consideration led Carl Christ to construct an index of rates paid on money substitutes. Although this approach is far superior to one which completely neglects these rates, it still does not enable one to distinguish the separate substitution effects for different money substitutes.[2] The problem of multicollinearity can in large part be avoided by the use of cross-sectional data, an approach which is further explored in Chapter 3.

The preceding considerations suggest that a useful approach to the definitional problem is to define money narrowly, but to take explicit account of all the variables which are believed to affect the demand for money so defined. Theoretical models involving the money concept consider the quantity of money as a policy variable; thus on the supply side the definition may include currency, demand deposits, and time deposits in commercial banks. As long as a stable demand function exists for any one of these assets, monetary policy can in principle be an effective tool for the control of economic activity. It is useful therefore to investigate the demand functions for particular assets separately, taking explicit account of the substitution relationships existing between other financial assets and the particular asset in question. If

---

[1] Richard T. Selden, "Monetary Velocity in the United States," in Milton Friedman (ed.), *Studies in the Quantity Theory of Money* (Chicago: University of Chicago Press, 1956), 179–257.

[2] Carl F. Christ, "Interest Rates and 'Portfolio Selection' Among Liquid Assets in the U.S.," in *Measurement in Economics: Studies in Mathematical Economics and Econometrics*, in Memory of Yehuda Grenfeld, Stanford University Press, 1963, pp. 201–18.

substitution relationships are empirically less significant than is usually assumed, it may be justifiable to neglect these assets altogether. This, however, is an empirical question which as yet has not been answered.

In order to isolate the substantive issues raised by recent critics of monetary policy, it is instructive to review the mechanism by which monetary policy affects target variables, such as income and the level of prices.

CHAPTER 2

The Monetary Mechanism

In a forthcoming paper, Friedman and Meiselman distinguish between the "credit" view and the "monetary" view of the effects of monetary policy.[1] The "credit" approach is most closely associated with the Keynesian liquidity preference analysis, which postulates that changes in the supply of money directly affect "the rate of interest" and thereby induce changes in the flow of investment expenditures which in turn affect the flow of income via the multiplier mechanism. The "monetary" view, on the other hand, focuses attention on the entire spectrum of explicit and implicit interest rates and regards a change in monetary policy as affecting the entire range of expenditures rather than the investment flows exclusively. As Friedman and Meiselman point out, the "crucial issue" in these alternative views of the operation of the monetary mechanism is "the *range* of interest rates, and accordingly, types of expenditures considered."

Both "monetary" and "credit" views of monetary policy are based on two fundamental, though often neglected, empirical assumptions. The first of these assumptions is that the demand for money is a stable function of a limited number of variables, such that the quantity of money demanded is a predictable magnitude. The second assumption, which both views of the monetary mechanism make, is that the demand for money and the supply of money are generally independent of one another or, more precisely, that the variables influencing the supply

---

[1] Milton Friedman and David Meiselman, "The Relative Stability of Monetary Velocity and the Investment Multiplier in the United States, 1897–1958." (Forthcoming publication of the Commission on Money and Credit.)

of money are independent of the variables influencing the demand for money. The critical role of the foregoing assumptions can best be illustrated by tracing through the effects of a monetary action.

Starting from an initial situation of equilibrium between actual and desired real cash balances, assume that the monetary authority wishes to stimulate the economy through an increase in the supply of money. The "credit" approach focuses attention on the change in "the rate of interest" which results from an initial change in the money supply. An increased supply of money presumably reduces "the rate of interest" (except in the special case of a liquidity trap), which increases the flow of income through the increase in investment expenditures. The reduction in "the rate of interest" is predictable if the monetary authorities have sufficient knowledge of the parameters of the demand function for money. The final change in income can be predicted if the interest elasticity of the investment function and the multiplier are known magnitudes. If an increase in the supply of money brought about an offsetting increase in the demand for money, then in the "credit" view, monetary policy could exert no pressure on the level of income, for "the rate of interest" would remain unchanged. Thus, if monetary policy is to be effective, (abstracting from the problem of lags) the demand for money must be a stable and predictable function, and the demand for money must be generally independent of the supply. Interdependence of demand and supply will reduce the effectiveness of any *given* policy action. If, however, the interdependence relationship is itself predictable, the monetary authorities could in principle still bring about the desired changes in the level of income or prices. Monetary policy would, of course, be impotent if changes in the money supply were *exactly* offset by changes in the demand for money.

The "monetary" view of monetary policy is somewhat different, although it, too, assumes that the demand for money is a predictable function and that the demand for money and the supply of money are independent. An increase in the supply of money will give each individual an incentive to readjust his asset portfolio in such a way as to rid himself of excess money balances. This readjustment is carried out by exchanging redundant money balances for other financial assets (lending) as well as purchasing goods and services (spending). Although any individual in the community can affect the quantity of nominal balances he holds, the community as a whole cannot affect the existing stock of nominal balances. In an effort to do so, however, the community can affect the quantity of real cash balances by bidding up the level of prices. The price effect will reduce the quantity of real balances and thus reduce the excess supply, whereas increases in real income can increase the demand for real cash balances and thus also help to eliminate excess supply. If the demand for money were highly unstable, the monetary authorities could not predict the outcome of any particular action, and if the demand for money and the supply were interdependent, such that an increase in the supply was immediately offset by increases in the demand, it would be impossible for the authorities to create a situation of excess supply, thereby rendering monetary policy ineffectual.

The most vocal critics of monetary policy have directly attacked the hypotheses that the demand for money is a stable function and that the demand for money and the supply of money are largely independent. John Gurley and Edward Shaw have voiced considerable concern about the effectiveness of monetary policy in a world of complex financial intermediation.[1] Gurley and Shaw base their analysis on the untested yet widely held hypothesis that the liabilities of non-bank financial intermediaries are close substitutes for money. The quantity of money demanded can in principle be affected by a large number of interest rates, and in particular by the rates of return on the liabilities of non-bank financial intermediaries. Gurley and Shaw correctly treat non-bank financial intermediaries as brokers of funds who utilize the law of large numbers to produce technological efficiencies in the funds market. Thus the basic effect of a financial intermediary is to reduce the spread between the borrower and the lender rate. The rapid growth of these financial intermediaries has increased the lender's rate of return, resulting in an increased opportunity cost of holding assets in the form of money. Gurley and Shaw conclude that the reduction in the demand for money resulting from changes in the quantity of other non-bank financial liabilities has led to a reduced effectiveness of any *given* monetary action.

If the monetary authorities can predict the changes in the quantity of money demanded (i.e., if the demand for money is a stable function of the rates of return on liabilities of financial intermediaries), then monetary policy will not be impaired by growth in financial intermediaries. Only if the demand function for money becomes less stable

---

[1] John Gurley and Edward Shaw, "Financial Aspects of Economic Development," *American Economic Review*, **XLV** (September, 1955), 515–38. "Financial Intermediaries and the Savings-Investment Process," *Journal of Finance*, **XI** (May, 1956), 257–76. *Money in a Theory of Finance*, Washington, 1960. "The Growth of Debt and Money in the United States, 1800–1950: A Suggested Interpretation," *Review of Economics and Statistics*, **XXXIX** (August, 1957), 250–62. "Agenda for a National Monetary Commission," —Discussion—see "Comment" by Gurley.

and therefore less predictable will monetary action be a less effective tool for economic stabilization. Moreover, if the liabilities of financial intermediaries are *not* close substitutes for money, the demand for money will be largely independent of changes in the rates of return on intermediary liabilities, and monetary control will not be impaired. As yet, Gurley and Shaw have not offered any empirical evidence which supports the notion that the liabilities of financial intermediaries are close substitutes for money as narrowly defined.

Gurley and Shaw do allude to the possibility that the growth of financial intermediaries has been accompanied by qualitative changes in the liabilities of financial intermediaries, which tend to make these liabilities more similar to the monetary asset. Qualitative changes in the liabilities of financial intermediaries can be analytically treated as changes in the preferences of individuals and can therefore be analyzed by applying the traditional theory of consumer behavior.[1]

Assuming a quadratic utility function,

$$(2.1) \qquad u = a_0 + \sum_{i=1}^{n} a_i q_i + \frac{1}{2} \sum_{i=1}^{n} \sum_{j=1}^{n} a_{ij} q_i q_j,$$

where $q_1, \ldots, q_n$ are regarded as the flows of non-pecuniary services rendered by assets $Q_1, \ldots, Q_n$, the marginal utilities are simply linear functions of the quantities, so that

$$(2.2) \qquad u_i = a_i + \sum_{j=1}^{n} a_{ij} q_j \qquad (i = 1, \ldots, n)$$

and the second derivatives of u are constants: $u_{ij} = a_{ij}$. A change in the quality of a particular liquid asset can be regarded as a change in the marginal utility of the non-pecuniary service flow which is independent of the quantities consumed. The effect of such a qualitative change on the quantities consumed can be found by differentiating the $(n + 1)$ first-order maximum conditions with respect to the change in quality. This differentiation yields,

$$(2.3) \qquad \frac{\partial q_i}{\partial a_j} = -\frac{X_{ji}}{\lambda},$$

where X_{ji} is the substitution term in the well-known Slutsky equation and λ is a Lagrange multiplier. Since substitutes are defined by the

---

[1] H. Theil, *Economic Forecasts and Policy* (Amsterdam: North-Holland Publishing Company, 1958), 400–402.

condition that $X_{ji} > 0$, and complements are defined by the condition that $X_{ji} < 0$, it follows that an increase in the quality of the non-pecuniary service flows rendered by the jth asset will increase the demand for the services of the ith asset if i and j are complements and reduce the demand for the services of the ith asset if i and j are substitutes.

Since the liabilities of financial intermediaries are usually regarded as substitutes for money, as narrowly defined, an increase in the quality of these liabilities can have the effect of reducing the demand for money and changing the parameters of the demand function for money. If the monetary authorities could predict quality changes and their effects on the demand for money, such changes would not impair the effectiveness of monetary action; as an empirical fact, however, it is doubtful that we can attribute such knowledge to the monetary authorities. Thus it is distinctly possible that substantial changes in quality can reduce the stability and thereby the predictability of the demand for money. If the growth of financial intermediaries were accompanied by changes in the quality of financial assets, monetary policy could become a less effective tool of economic management.

The Gurley-Shaw thesis also attacks the assumption that the demand for money and the supply of money are independent. Gurley and Shaw argue that a tight monetary policy can induce financial innovation which changes the qualitative characteristics of the liabilities of financial intermediaries, making the intermediary liabilities more similar to monetary assets held by individuals. Since an increase in the quality of financial intermediary liabilities can have the effect of reducing the demand for money, a tight monetary policy will lose some of its leverage effect. If the reduction in the demand for money partially offsets the reduction in the money supply, any *given* policy action will be less effective. If, however, the authorities could predict the corresponding decrease in the quantity of money demanded, they could pursue a more vigorous policy which would achieve their final objective. On the other hand, if the reduction in the quantity of money demanded cannot be predicted by the policy makers, the consequences of any particular monetary action will be less predictable and therefore less effective as a stabilization measure.

Although Gurley and Shaw suggest that financial intermediation may reduce the stability of the demand for money, and that induced financial innovation may operate to make the supply of money and the demand for money interdependent, their conclusions regarding the effectiveness of monetary policy ultimately depend upon the following untested empirical propositions:

1. The quantity of money demanded is significantly affected by the rates of return on the liabilities of financial intermediaries; i.e., the liabilities of financial intermediaries are close substitutes for money.

2. The substitution relationships are unstable or, more generally, unpredictable.

3. The growth of financial intermediaries has been accompanied by qualitative changes in the characteristics of the financial intermediaries' liabilities which have had the effect of reducing the stability of the parameters of the demand function for money.

4. Tight monetary policy has the effect of inducing financial innovation which reduces the demand for money and reduces the stability of the parameters of the demand functions for money.

The foregoing propositions will be tested in the following chapter by deriving estimates of the demand functions for demand deposits, time deposits, and savings and loan association shares and by testing the parameters and the stability of these functions.

CHAPTER 3

Estimation of Demand Functions for Financial Assets

Variables Affecting the Demand for Financial Assets

Many financial assets are described as being *liquid*. The adjective *liquid* refers to a particular non-pecuniary service flow rendered by this particular subset of assets. Other non-pecuniary services may include salability, safety, convenience, defense against misfortune, etc. When one considers the demand for such assets, the relevant relationship involves the bundle of non-pecuniary service flows rendered by these assets. The emphasis on flows, rather than on stocks, permits utilization of the analytic framework provided by the traditional theory of consumer behavior.

The theory of consumer behavior classifies those variables which affect the individual's demand for a particular commodity. The traditional demand hypothesis asserts that the demand for a commodity depends upon the price of the commodity, income, the prices of related commodities, and tastes. Analogously, the demand for the non-pecuniary services of an asset depends upon the price of the services, income, prices of related services, and tastes. The problem then is to define the quantity dimensions of the service flows, the prices of these flows, and to specify the other related variables.

A given stock of a financial asset yields a stream of various non-

16

pecuniary services. One may define the quantity dimension of this stream in terms of the dollar value of the stock that yields the services, so that one can speak of the services per unit time rendered by a dollar of a particular financial asset. The appropriate price of the service is the number of dollars required to buy the particular service stream, per unit time, of a dollar's worth of the asset. Although the value of the service stream cannot be observed, the value of the stock is directly measurable. Assuming a fixed relationship between the stock and the flow of services rendered by the given stock permits utilization of the stock quantity as a proxy measure of the flow. We can thus use the terms *the demand for a financial asset* and the *demand for the non-pecuniary services* yielded by a financial asset interchangeably.

The price of the service flow rendered by a particular asset is the alternative income foregone by purchasing a specific service flow. This price is the difference between the pecuniary return of an asset which yields no non-pecuniary service and the net pecuniary return on the asset in question. Thus, if these returns are expressed as a fraction of the value of the asset,

$$(3.1) \qquad\qquad P_i = r_0 - r_i^n,$$

where P_i is the price of the non-pecuniary service rendered by the ith asset, r_0 is the pecuniary rate of return on an asset yielding no non-pecuniary services, and r_i^n is the net pecuniary rate of return on the ith asset. If r_0 is considered fixed, the price of the service flow rendered by the ith asset varies inversely with the net pecuniary return on the ith asset.

The net pecuniary rate of return on the ith asset equals the sum of all pecuniary returns, minus the costs associated with the acquisition of the asset and its yield. For convenience, these costs and returns can be expressed as a fraction of the value of the asset so that,

$$(3.2) \qquad\qquad r_i^n = r_i^i + r_i^g - r_i^c,$$

where r_i^i is the pecuniary interest return per dollar per year, r_i^g is the non-interest pecuniary return per dollar per year (this may include additional gifts and premiums which are distributed with some assets), and r_i^c is the acquisition cost per dollar per year.

The asset holder's behavior will be influenced by the net pecuniary rates of return on other assets. If the rate of return on an asset increases, the individual has an incentive to rearrange his asset portfolio in such a way as to substitute this asset for other assets whose relative yields are lower.

The income of the asset holder will affect the total stock of assets desired as well as the mix of particular assets in his portfolio.

The foregoing classification of variables suggested by consumer theory can be regarded as a hypothesis which specifies that the demand for a particular liquid asset will depend upon the interest return on the asset, the interest returns on alternative assets, non-interest pecuniary returns, convenience costs associated with the acquisition of assets, income, and tastes.

In order to estimate the demand functions for liquid assets, it is desirable to choose a sample with the following attributes: the variables measured should correspond to those postulated by the theoretical model; the sample size should be large enough to permit statistical inferences; the observed quantities should exhibit sufficient variation to provide a basis for the inferences desired. Cross-sectional state data for the United States provide these desirable sample characteristics. State data were collected for the eleven-year period 1949–59. Each year provides a cross-sectional sample of 49 observations, taken from the then 48 states plus the District of Columbia.

Measurement of the Variables

Quantity Variables. In order to estimate demand functions for liquid assets held by *individuals*, it is desirable to derive measures of quantity which exclude the holdings of partnerships, corporations, and state, local, and Federal governments. Data for individual holdings of demand deposits, time deposits, and savings and loan association shares cannot be obtained directly. The finest available breakdown of deposits by ownership class is the sum of deposits held by individuals, partnerships, and corporations.

Because corporations and partnerships hold a small fraction of time deposits and savings and loan association shares, the individual, corporation, and partnership ownership classification is a close approximation to the desired measure of individual holdings, and no additional adjustment seems warranted.

For demand deposits, the aggregation of corporation and partnership balances with individual balances poses a more serious problem. The Federal deposit ownership survey indicates that almost 50 per cent of commercial bank demand deposits are held by corporations. If the demand functions for corporate balances and individual balances were very similar, use of the aggregated balances as the dependent variable would not significantly alter the estimates of the structural parameters. If, on the other hand, the demand functions for individual and corporate balances differed substantially, use of aggregative balances could yield distorted estimates of the structural parameters of the individual demand functions.

In order to reduce the possible error stemming from the inclusion of business balances, an adjustment of the deposit figures has been attempted, to separate out the individual holdings. For the past few years, the Federal Reserve Board has conducted an ownership survey of demand deposit holdings throughout the United States. Although this survey was designed to provide national estimates, it was possible to estimate individuals' holdings on a state basis from the 1960 survey data. Estimates of the fraction of total deposits held by individuals in each state were computed from the original survey data. It was assumed that the fraction of total deposits held by individuals varies considerably more among states than over time for a given state: the state ratios derived from the 1960 survey were therefore included as an independent variable in the demand deposit equation for the 1949–59 period. Because the ownership survey was not designed for this particular type of breakdown, it is difficult to estimate the reliability of this variable.

Interest Returns. The interest returns on time deposits, mutual savings bank deposits, and savings and loan association shares can be measured by taking either the announced nominal rate of return or the actual interest rate paid. The two rates differ because of institutional arrangements regarding compounding of interest and different payment schedules. Since the actual rate represents more clearly the real market opportunities affecting the consumer, this is the rate used in the analysis. The actual interest rate is computed by dividing the total interest payments in a particular period (derived from the consolidated income and expense data of the various institutions) by the average balance of the assets held during the period. The same procedure is used with regard to demand deposits: in this case, however, the interest return is negative and is represented by total service charges divided by average demand deposit balances for the period.

Non-interest Returns. Non-interest returns, such as gifts and premiums offered by savings and loan associations, have become commonplace in the postwar period as a method of attracting new depositors. Since these returns affect the attractiveness of savings and loan association shares, they should be included in the demand function. Unfortunately, it is impossible to estimate accurately the amounts of such non-interest returns, because they are included in the income and expense statements under the general category of advertising expenditures. Although some commercial banks, as well as some mutual savings banks, utilize this method of increasing the effective return, the practice has been carried out on a large scale only by savings and loan associations. Recent literature attributes the rapid growth in savings and loan associations in the postwar period in part to their aggressive advertising policies. Advertising expenditures are therefore included in the demand function for savings and loan association shares in order to test this particular hypothesis as well as clearly to specify the market opportunities facing individual consumers. Advertising expenditures of savings and loan associations were also included as a variable in the demand functions for demand deposits and time deposits. The parameters of the advertising variable did not differ significantly from zero in the preliminary estimates; therefore the variable was excluded from the demand deposit and time deposit equations in the final analysis.

Convenience Costs. The costs associated with the acquisition of a particular asset and its service yield may vary among states. Since the major convenience cost appears to be the value of the individual's time spent in acquiring an asset or utilizing the non-pecuniary services of the asset, a proxy variable for convenience cost was considered for inclusion in the analysis. The per capita number of offices of commercial banks, savings and loan associations, and mutual savings banks was introduced as arguments of the demand functions for the various assets considered. The preliminary regression results indicated that the parameters of these variables were not significantly different from zero when regional shift variables were included in the analysis. The role of convenience costs in affecting the demand for liquid assets, however, deserves further explicit investigation.

Income. Personal income data are available on a state basis. The personal income data were adjusted in order to derive a series of "permanent personal income." *Permanent personal income* is a weighted average of present and past values of personal income; the weights are adopted from Friedman's study of the consumption function.[1] The

---

[1] Milton Friedman, *A Theory of the Consumption Function* (Princeton: Princeton University Press, 1957).

"permanent" and the "measured" series are highly correlated because the Department of Commerce obtained the estimates of personal income by states by using interpolation between benchmark years.

Single Equation Least Squares Estimation

In a particular year, the $S \times 1$ vector y describes the collection of observations on the per capita quantity of liquid asset y in the S states where $s = 1, 2, \ldots, 49$. Similarly, the $S \times j$ matrix X describes a collection of observations on a set of independent variables, J in number, observed in the S states. The observations are assumed to be generated in the following fashion:

$$(3.3) \qquad y = X\beta + e,$$

where β is a $J \times 1$ coefficient vector and e is a $S \times 1$ vector of disturbances. A typical equation in the system is

$$(3.4) \qquad y_s = \beta_1 x_{1s} + \beta_2 x_{2s} +, \ldots, + \beta_j x_{js} + e_s.$$

The demand functions for various liquid assets are estimated by the method of least squares, from the cross-sectional sample previously described. The derived regression estimates are based on the following assumptions:

1. The form of the demand functions is linear and the slope coefficients of the variables included in the demand function for a particular liquid asset are the same for all states.

2. The intercepts of the demand functions for a particular liquid asset can vary among geographic areas and among states with important financial centers. Dummy variables were included in the X matrix such that each of the geographic areas (West, South, Central, Northeast) and each of the states which contain the main financial centers of the respective geographic area (California, Washington, D.C., Illinois, New York) was allowed a free intercept.

3. The level of the supply curve of a particular asset differs between states, and is independent of the variables which shift the demand curve. The level of the supply curve in each state is determined primarily by state laws and regulations governing the

activities of financial intermediaries. The rates of return are therefore considered as exogenous variables.

4. Consumer behavior in any given state is affected only by economic conditions in that state.

The notations and definitions of the variables used in the estimation procedure are as follows:

Notation	*Definition*
D	Per capita commercial bank demand deposits held by individuals, partnerships, and corporations
T	Per capital commercial bank time deposits
S	Per capita savings and loan association shares
Y	"Permanent" per capita personal income
r_d	Actual interest rate on commercial bank demand deposits (negative)
r_t	Actual interest rate on commercial bank time deposits
r_s	Actual interest rate on savings and loan association shares
r_m	Actual interest rate on mutual savings bank deposits
D_m	Dummy variable (1 for mutual savings bank states, 0 for non-mutual savings bank states)
I	Survey estimate of the ratio of commercial bank demand deposits held by individuals to total commercial bank demand deposits
A	Per capita advertising expenditures by savings and loan associations
Cal	Dummy variable (1 for California; 0 for all other states)
DC	Dummy variable (1 for Washington, D.C.; 0 for all other states)
Ill	Dummy variable (1 for Illinois; 0 for all other states)
NY	Dummy variable (1 for New York; 0 for all other states)
W	Dummy variable (1 for Western states excluding California; 0 for all other states)
S	Dummy variable (1 for Southern states excluding Washington, D.C.; 0 for all other states)
C	Dummy variable (1 for Central states excluding Illinois; 0 for all other states)
NE	Dummy variable (1 for Northeastern states excluding New York; 0 for all other states)

Single Equation Least Squares Estimates—
Demand Deposits

The single equation least squares estimates of the demand functions for demand deposits for the individual years 1949–59 are listed in Table 4 in Appendix A. A summary of the own price and cross substitution terms is found in Table 7 and the estimated elasticities are listed in Table 8. The Durbin-Watson statistic was computed for each of the equations in order to test the functional form implied by (3.4).[1] In each of the eleven equations, it was impossible to reject the hypothesis that the linear form implied by (3.4) was the correct specification.

The coefficients of income in all the equations are highly significant.[2] The income elasticities (estimated at the respective means) do not significantly differ from unity. The coefficients of the interest rate on demand deposits are significant and have the expected sign for all years. These coefficients imply that a reduction in service charges will significantly increase the quantity of demand deposits demanded.

The coefficients of the interest rates on time deposits and savings and loan association shares do not differ significantly from zero, implying that these assets are not as substitutable for demand deposits as has been assumed in much of the monetary literature.

The relationship between demand deposits and mutual savings bank deposits is somewhat ambiguous. The coefficients of the mutual savings bank rate are positive, implying a complementary relationship between demand deposits and mutual savings bank deposits. The coefficient of the mutual savings bank dummy variable is, on the other hand, significantly negative. These results may be interpreted as implying a short-run complementary relationship, but a long-run substitution relationship between demand deposits and mutual savings bank deposits.

The coefficients of the geographic areas and the coefficients of financial centers with the exception of New York do not differ significantly from zero. The New York coefficients are positive and significant, as might be expected, owing to the errors of measurement in the dependent variable for the New York observation.

---

[1] See S. Prais and H. Houthakker, *The Analysis of Family Budgets* (Cambridge: The University Press, 1955), 51–53; also J. Durbin and G. S. Watson, "Testing for Serial Correlation in Least Squares Regression," *Biometrika*, **XXXVIII** (1951), 159–78.

[2] The .05 level was selected as the criterion for all significance tests.

The most remarkable feature of the estimated demand functions is the apparent stability of the coefficients over the time period considered. It is possible to test the stability of the demand functions over the entire time period by computing a pooled regression which constrains the coefficients to be equal over time. The sum of squared errors from the pooled regression can be compared to the sum of the sum of squared errors from the individual year regressions in order to test the hypothesis that the demand functions were stable over the period.[1] The appropriate F-statistic,

$$F \, p(K - 1) \, (n - pK) \; = \; .705,$$

where p is the number of independent variables, K the number of categories (years), and n the number of observations in the sample. The test indicates that one cannot reject the hypothesis that the demand functions were stable over the time period considered. This latter result implies that financial innovation had no significant effect on reducing the stability of the demand function for demand deposits in the time period considered.

Pooling the individual cross sections for the entire period 1949–59, and constraining the coefficients to be constant over time, yielded the following regression equation:

$$D = .365 \; Y + 535 \; r_d - 35 \; r_t + 53 \; r_s + 25 \; r_m - 126 \; D_m + 405 \; I$$
$$ (.080) \qquad (48) \qquad (13) \qquad (13) \qquad (15) \qquad (34) \qquad (71)$$

$$+ \; 4 \; \text{Cal} + 283 \; \text{DC} + 151 \; \text{Ill} + 734 \; \text{NY} + 10 \; \text{W}$$
$$ (57) \qquad (55) \qquad (48) \qquad (48) \qquad (43)$$

$$- \; 103 \; \text{S} + .2 \; \text{C} - 32 \; \text{NE}.$$
$$ (42) \qquad (43) \qquad (45)$$

The coefficient of multiple determination adjusted for degrees of freedom is .978. The own price elasticity, the cross-elasticities, and the income elasticity (all estimated at the means) are listed on the first line of Table 1.

The results of the pooled single equation least squares estimates may be summarized as follows:

    1. The income elasticity of demand deposits does not differ significantly from unity.

---

[1] This test is described by S. Kullback and H. M. Rosenblatt, "On the Analysis of Multiple Regression in k Categories," *Biometrika*, **XLIV** (1957), 67–83.

TABLE 1. MATRIX OF OWN PRICE, CROSS AND INCOME ELASTICITIES

Pooled Single Equation Least Squares Estimates

1949–59

	Elasticity Estimates at the Mean				
Dependent variable	η_{xd}	η_{xt}	η_{xs}	η_{xm}	η_{xy}
Demand deposits	−.31	.10	−.30	−.04	.92
Time deposits	.13	−.49	.55	.28	.69
Savings and loan association shares	.10	.003	−.18	.08	.63

2. The own price coefficient is more than ten times its standard error and suggests that increases in the service charges on demand deposits will substantially reduce the quantity of demand deposits demanded.

3. Demand deposits and time deposits in commercial banks appear to be weak substitutes.

4. Demand deposits and savings and loan association shares appear to be complements in the pooled equation although the individual cross-section regressions indicate that the two assets are roughly independent in demand.

The possibility of finding complementarity relationships among liquid assets has been suggested by Tobin and Brainard, who argue that an increase in the rate of return on the liabilities of a financial intermediary may have the direct effect of reducing individuals' demand for demand deposits, but the indirect effect of increasing the demand for demand deposits as reserves for the intermediary.[1]

If the indirect effect outweighs the direct effect, complementarity rather than substitution will be observed. As Tobin and Brainard state: "Even though the substitution assumption applies to the portfolio choices of the public, and of every intermediary, taken separately, it is possible that assets will be complements in the systems as a whole. This can happen whenever the public and intermediaries hold the same

---

[1] J. Tobin and W. C. Brainard, "Financial Intermediaries and the Effectiveness of Monetary Controls." Unpublished paper delivered at the meetings of the Econometric Society, December, 1962.

assets or whenever one intermediary holds as assets the liabilities of another intermediary."

Since it was not possible completely to separate individual holdings of demand deposits from holdings of financial intermediaries, it is possible that this error of measurement in the dependent variable accounts for the complementarity result. It is interesting to note that the pooled single equation least squares estimate of the demand function for savings and loan association shares indicates that demand deposits and savings and loan association shares are weak substitutes. Both the complementarity result from the demand deposit equation and the substitution result from the savings and loan association equations are consistent with the Tobin-Brainard hypothesis. The savings and loan demand function is not subject to the measurement error found in the demand deposit equation and thus suggests that demand deposits and savings and loan deposits are weak substitutes in the asset portfolios of individuals. The complementarity result from the demand deposit equation implies that the indirect effect of an increase in the rate of return on savings and loan association shares outweighed the direct effect, since the demand for demand deposits on the part of savings and loan associations is included in the measurement of the dependent variable.

5. Mutual savings bank deposits and demand deposits appear to be independent in the short run and substitutes in the long run. The weak complementary relationship between mutual savings deposits and demand deposits may be explained by a hypothesis similar to that previously described.

Single Equation Least Squares Estimates—Time Deposits

The single equation least squares estimates of the demand functions for time deposits for the individual years 1949–59 are listed in Table 5. The own price and cross substitution terms are summarized in Table 7, and the elasticities estimated at the means are listed in Table 8.

The Durbin-Watson statistic was employed to test the functional form, and the test revealed no significant departures from linearity.

The coefficients of the time deposit equations were tested for stability over time, and it was not possible to reject the hypothesis that the demand functions were stable over the time period. The appropriate F-statistic was,

$$F\ (p(k\ -\ 1)\ (n\ -\ pk)\ =\ .555.$$

Pooling the individual cross sections for the entire period 1949–59, and constraining the coefficients to be constant over time yielded the following regression equation:

$$T = .122 \ Y - 101 \ r_d + 76 \ r_t - 44 \ r_s - 82 \ r_m + 235 \ D_m$$
$$(.037) \qquad (37) \qquad (10) \qquad (10) \qquad (11) \qquad (25)$$

$$+ \ 304 \ \text{Cal} + 86 \ \text{DC} + 204 \ \text{Ill} + 69 \ \text{NY} + 39 \ \text{W}$$
$$(40) \qquad (39) \qquad (35) \qquad (32) \qquad (28)$$

$$+ \ 7 \ \text{S} + 57 \ \text{C} + 57 \ \text{NE.}$$
$$(27) \qquad (27) \qquad (27)$$

The coefficient of multiple determination adjusted for degrees of freedom is .942. The own price elasticity, the cross elasticities, and the income elasticity are listed on the second line of Table 1.

The results of the pooled single equation least squares estimates may be summarized as follows:

1. The income elasticity of time deposits is .69, which is considerably lower than the income elasticity estimated for demand deposits. Inspection of Table 8 reveals that the income elasticity
   of time deposits was greater than the income elasticity of demand
   deposits in the early years of the period, but dropped sharply in
   the later years. This result sheds some light on the recent discussion concerning the income elasticity of the demand for money.

Milton Friedman has estimated a demand function for money and concludes that the income elasticity of the demand for money is approximately 1.8, implying that money is a "luxury" asset.[1] Friedman's estimates of the income elasticity are not strictly comparable to those of the present study insofar as different definitions of *money* and *income* were used in the two studies. Friedman's money series included time deposits in addition to currency and demand deposits, and Friedman's income series was adjusted net national product as opposed to the personal income series utilized in the present study. Friedman's inclusion of currency would tend to have the effect of reducing his income elasticity estimate, for Philip Cagen has demonstrated that the income elasticity of currency is less than that of demand deposits.[2]

---

[1] Milton Friedman, "The Demand for Money: Some Theoretical and Empirical Results," National Bureau of Economic Research, *Occasional Paper* 68, 1959.

[2] Philip Cagen, "The Demand for Currency Relative to the Total Money Supply," *Journal of Political Economy*, **LXVI** (August, 1958), 303–28.

The results listed in Table 8 suggest that the income elasticity of time deposits exceeded the income elasticity of demand deposits from 1949–53. If the income elasticity of time deposits had been substantially higher than that of demand deposits and currency in the period prior to 1949, the inclusion of time deposits in the definition of money may have been responsible for Friedman's high income elasticity. The period from 1954–59 shows a marked decline in the income elasticity of time deposits, and this might also explain why Friedman's demand function does a poor job of predicting the demand for money in this latter period.

2. The own price coefficient of time deposits is more than seven times its standard error and implies that an increase in the rate of return on time deposits will substantially increase the demand for time deposits. The interest elasticity estimated at the means is approximately +.50, implying an own price elasticity of −.50.

This result helps to clarify some of the apparent conflicts in the findings of various economists who have estimated demand functions for money, using different definitions of money. Friedman's findings suggest that the demand for money (defined as currency plus demand deposits plus time deposits in commercial banks) depends primarily upon income and is unaffected by changes in the rate of interest.[1] Latané, on the other hand, suggests that the rate of interest has a significant impact on the demand for money (defined as currency plus demand deposits).[2] Carl Christ in re-estimating Latané's demand function for money found that the interest rate impact was significantly reduced when time deposits were included in the definition of money.[3]

These apparently conflicting results can be reconciled by recognizing the dual role played by the rate of interest. When money is defined narrowly, the rate of interest represents the opportunity cost of holding money and the coefficient of the interest rate in the demand function for money narrowly defined is expected to be negative. Latané's estimate of this interest elasticity is approximately −.50. The interest rate, however, also assumes the role of a proxy variable for the yield on time deposits, and the estimate of the own interest elasticity for time deposits has been shown to be approximately +.50. Thus when money is defined to include time deposits, the two separate effects are likely to

---

[1] Milton Friedman, *op. cit.*

[2] H. A. Latané, *op. cit.*

[3] Carl F. Christ, *op. cit.*

be offsetting, resulting in a weak or insignificant relationship between the rate of interest and money broadly defined.

3. Demand deposits and time deposits appear to be substitutes, implying that an increase in service charges on demand deposits will increase the demand for time deposits. The cross elasticity estimated from the time deposit equation is .13, and does not differ significantly from the cross elasticity estimated from the demand deposit equation. The individual cross-section regressions indicate that demand deposits and time deposits are very weak substitutes and that the degree of substitutability declined over time.

4. The pooled regression equation implies that time deposits and savings and loan association shares are substitutes.

5. Mutual savings bank deposits and time deposits appear to be short-run substitutes.

Single Equation Least Squares Estimates—Savings and Loan Association Shares

The single equation least squares estimates of the demand functions for savings and loan association shares for the individual years 1949–59 are listed in Table 6. The own price and cross substitution terms are summarized in Table 7 and the elasticities estimated at the means are listed in Table 8.

The Durbin-Watson statistic was employed to test the functional form, and the test revealed no significant departures from linearity.

The coefficients of the savings and loan association demand functions were tested for stability over time, and it was not possible to reject the hypothesis that the demand functions were stable over time. The savings and loan demand functions, however, exhibit less stability than the demand functions for demand deposits and time deposits, implying that qualitative changes in the characteristics of the savings and loan association liabilities may have had some effect on reducing the stability of the demand functions over time. The value of the F-statistic employed in the stability test was

$$F \, p(k-1)(n-pk) \ = \ 1.14.$$

Pooling the individual cross sections for the entire period 1949–59, and constraining the coefficients to be constant over time yielded the following regression equation:

$$S = .069\ Y - 48\ r_d + .25\ r_t + 9\ r_s - 14\ r_m + 66\ D_m + .48\ A$$
$$(.008)\quad (19)\quad\ \ (5.39)\quad (5)\quad\ \ (6)\quad\ \ (14)\quad\ \ (.01)$$

$$- 177\ \text{Cal} + 125\ \text{DC} - 128\ \text{Ill} - 118\ \text{NY} - 114\ \text{W}$$
$$\ \ (21)\qquad\ \ (21)\qquad\ (18)\qquad (17)\qquad (15)$$

$$- 69\ \text{S} - 94\ \text{C} - 116\ \text{NE.}$$
$$\ (14)\quad\ \ (14)\quad\ \ (16)$$

The coefficient of multiple determination adjusted for degrees of freedom is .968. The own price elasticity, the cross elasticities, and the income elasticity are listed on the third line of Table 1.

The results of the pooled single equation least squares estimates may be summarized as follows:

1. The income elasticity of savings and loan association shares appears to be very similar to that of time deposits and less than the income elasticity of demand deposits.

2. The own price coefficient has the expected sign, but the own price elasticity of savings and loan association shares is substantially lower than the own price elasticities of demand and time deposits.

3. Demand deposits and savings and loan association shares appear to be weak substitutes, but the substitution relationship appears to have strengthened over time.

4. Savings and loan association shares and time deposits appear to be independent of one another.

5. The demand for savings and loan association shares appears to be most strongly affected by the per capita advertising expenditures of savings and loan associations. The advertising coefficient is highly significant for all cross sections and is fifty times its standard error in the pooled regression.

A possible explanation for this significant relationship is that a supply rather than a demand phenomenon is observed in the regression coefficients. Assume, for example, that savings and loan associations determined the size of their advertising budget by a rule of thumb, which allocated a fixed percentage of total shares outstanding to advertising expenditures. If such a practice prevailed, the highly significant coefficient of per capita advertising expenditures would be misleading, in that it would reflect a supply phenomenon. In order to test this possible explanation, advertising expenditures were deflated by average savings and loan association shares outstanding, and the regressions recomputed. If the significant relationship between per capita advertising expenditures and savings and loan association shares was purely a supply phenomenon, one would expect a coefficient equal to zero for the adjusted advertising variable in the recomputed regression. The resulting regression indicated a coefficient which was positive and highly significant in all cross sections. This test suggests that the significant relationship observed in the original regression is indeed a demand phenomenon. It must be recalled that advertising expenditures include such items as gifts and premiums doled out by the associations. The results indicate that gifts and premiums in addition to the informational services provided by advertising have a significant effect on the demand for savings and loan association shares.

It is interesting to note that advertising expenditures by savings and loan associations had no significant effect on the demand for demand deposits and time deposits. This result, coupled with the weak substitution coefficients derived from the savings and loan association equations, suggests that demand deposits and time deposits are not as close substitutes for savings and loan association shares as it is usually assumed. The significant advertising coefficient in the savings and loan association demand equation suggests that assets other than demand deposits and time deposits have been substituted for savings and loan association shares.

Efficient Estimation of the Demand Functions for Liquid Assets

The data described in the preceding section lend themselves to an estimation procedure developed by Arnold Zellner which yields coefficient estimators which are asymptotically more efficient than single equation least squares estimators.[1]

The demand function for a particular asset may be considered as a single equation from a system of equations consisting of demand func-

---

[1] Arnold Zellner, "An Efficient Method of Estimating Seemingly Unrelated Regressions and Tests for Aggregation Bias," *Journal of American Statistical Association*, LVII (June, 1962), 348–68. The estimates presented in this section were computed from a Fortran program developed by Arnold Zellner and Arthur Stroud at the University of Wisconsin.

tions for various assets. Thus one may regard

(3.5)
$$y_\mu = X_\mu \beta_\mu + e_\mu$$

as the μth equation of an M equation regression system with y_μ a $S \times 1$ vector of observations on the μth asset, X_μ a $S \times j$ matrix of observations on the J "independent" variables, β_μ a $J \times 1$ vector of regression coefficients, and e_μ a $S \times 1$ vector of random disturbances. The system of which (3.5) is an equation may be written as

(3.6)
$$
\begin{bmatrix} y_1 \\ y_2 \\ \cdot \\ \cdot \\ \cdot \\ y_M \end{bmatrix}
=
\begin{bmatrix} X_1 & 0 & \cdots & 0 \\ 0 & X_2 & \cdots & 0 \\ \cdot & \cdot & & \cdot \\ \cdot & \cdot & & \cdot \\ \cdot & \cdot & & \cdot \\ 0 & 0 & \cdots & X_M \end{bmatrix}
\begin{bmatrix} \beta_1 \\ \beta_2 \\ \cdot \\ \cdot \\ \cdot \\ \beta_M \end{bmatrix}
+
\begin{bmatrix} e_1 \\ e_2 \\ \cdot \\ \cdot \\ \cdot \\ e_M \end{bmatrix} ;
$$

(3.7)
$$y = X\beta + e,$$

where $y \equiv [y_1', y_2', \ldots, y_M']'$, $\beta \equiv [\beta_1', \beta_2', \ldots, \beta_M']'$, $e \equiv [e_1', e_2', \ldots, e_M']'$, and X is the block-diagonal matrix of (3.6).

The $M \times 1$ disturbance vector of (3.7) is assumed to have the following variance-covariance matrix.

(3.8)
$$
\Sigma = V(e) =
\begin{bmatrix}
\sigma_{11}I & \sigma_{12}I & \cdots & \sigma_{1M}I \\
\sigma_{21}I & \sigma_{22}I & \cdots & \sigma_{2M}I \\
\cdot & & & \\
\cdot & & & \\
\cdot & & & \\
\sigma_{M1}I & \sigma_{M2}I & \cdots & \sigma_{MM}I
\end{bmatrix}
$$

$$
=
\begin{bmatrix}
\sigma_{11} & \sigma_{12} & \cdots & \sigma_{1M} \\
\sigma_{21} & \sigma_{22} & \cdots & \sigma_{2M} \\
\cdot & & & \\
\cdot & & & \\
\cdot & & & \\
\sigma_{M1} & \sigma_{M2} & \cdots & \sigma_{MM}
\end{bmatrix}
\cdot I,
$$

where I is a $S \times S$ unit matrix and $\sigma'_{\mu\mu} = E(e_{\mu s} e_{\mu' s})$ for $s = 1, \ldots, S$ and $\mu, \mu' = 1, \ldots, M$.

For the data described in the preceding section, (3.6) reduces to

$$
(3.9) \qquad
\begin{bmatrix} y_d \\ y_t \\ y_{\tilde{s}} \end{bmatrix}
=
\begin{bmatrix} X_d & 0 & 0 \\ 0 & X_t & 0 \\ 0 & 0 & X_{\tilde{s}} \end{bmatrix}
\begin{bmatrix} \beta_d \\ \beta_t \\ \beta_{\tilde{s}} \end{bmatrix}
+
\begin{bmatrix} e_d \\ e_t \\ e \end{bmatrix},
$$

where the subscripts d, t, $\tilde{s}$, refer respectively to the assets, demand deposits, time deposits, and savings and loan association shares. The variance-covariance matrix (3.8) reduces to

$$
(3.10) \qquad \Sigma = V(e) =
\begin{bmatrix}
\sigma_{dd}I & \sigma_{dt}I & \sigma_{d\tilde{s}}I \\
\sigma_{td}I & \sigma_{tt}I & \sigma_{t\tilde{s}}I \\
\sigma_{\tilde{s}d}I & \sigma_{\tilde{s}t}I & \sigma_{\tilde{s}\tilde{s}}I
\end{bmatrix}
=
\begin{bmatrix}
\sigma_{dd} & \sigma_{dt} & \sigma_{ds} \\
\sigma_{td} & \sigma_{tt} & \sigma_{ts} \\
\sigma_{\tilde{s}d} & \sigma_{\tilde{s}t} & \sigma_{\tilde{s}\tilde{s}}
\end{bmatrix}
\cdot I.
$$

The form of (3.10) is such that there are correlations between the disturbances or dependent variables relating to a particular state, but no such correlations are assumed to exist among states. Moreover, the form of (3.10) implies that disturbance variances and covariances are assumed to be constant from state to state.

Given the regression system in (3.9), it is possible to construct the "pure" Aitken estimator of the coefficient vector which is

$$
(3.11) \qquad b^* = (X' \, \Sigma^{-1} \, X)^{-1} X' \, \Sigma^{-1} \, y
$$

and its covariance matrix,

$$
(3.12) \qquad V(b^*) = (X' \, \Sigma^{-1} \, X)^{-1}.
$$

As Σ is generally unknown, an estimate of the disturbance variance-covariance matrix is formed from the single equation least squares residuals. The resulting estimator of β has the property of being asymptotically more efficient than the single equation least squares estimator. The gain in efficiency occurs because the Aitken estimator of the coefficients of a single equation takes account of the zero restrictions on the coefficients of the other equations. If the non-zero submatrices of X in (3.6) are all equal; that is, $X_1 = X_2 = \ldots = X_M$, then the Aitken estimator reduces to the single equation least squares estimator.

The coefficients of the demand functions for demand deposits, time deposits, and savings and loan association shares, derived from the efficient estimation technique, are listed in Tables 9–11. The summaries of the own and cross price terms are listed in Table 12; and income, own price, and cross elasticities are listed in Table 13.

The resulting coefficients do not significantly differ from the single equation least squares estimates because the non-zero submatrices of X in (3.9) are nearly identical. As the demand for different liquid assets is affected by roughly the same set of independent variables, the number of zero restrictions implicit in (3.9) is substantially reduced, with the result that the potential gain in efficiency from the Aitken estimator cannot be exploited.

Restricted Efficient Estimation

The estimates of the demand functions derived in the preceding section suggest the possibility of subjecting the theory of rational consumers' behavior to empirical test. In particular, one may inquire whether or not the traditional theory of consumers' choice can be usefully applied to behavioral decisions regarding the choice of liquid assets. The theory of consumer choice postulates the familiar "Slutsky condition" that

$$(3.13) \qquad X_{ji} = \frac{\partial x_j}{\partial p_i} + x_i \frac{\partial x_j}{\partial Y} = \frac{\partial x_i}{\partial p_j} + x_j \frac{\partial x_i}{\partial Y} = X_{ij}.$$

This equation separates the effects of a change in the price of the non-pecuniary services rendered by the ith asset on the quantity demanded of the non-pecuniary services rendered by the jth asset into a income effect and a substitution effect, where X_{ji} represents the substitution effect, $-x_i \, \partial x_j/\partial Y$ represents the income effect, and the total effect is given by $\partial x_j/\partial p_i$. Traditional consumer theory postulates that the substitution effects of a change in the price of the ith service flow on the demand for the jth service is symmetrical with the substitution effect of a change in the price of the jth service flow on the demand for the ith service.

The simpler "Hotelling condition,"

$$(3.14) \qquad \frac{\partial x_j}{\partial p_i} = \frac{\partial x_i}{\partial p_j} = \frac{\partial x_j}{\partial (r_0 - r_i)} = \frac{\partial x_i}{\partial (r_0 - r_j)}$$

is approximately satisfied if the income effects are either negligible, as compared with the substitution effects, or are of equal importance for the service flows considered.

The theoretical conditions, (3.13) and (3.14), related to the demand of a single individual, whereas the statistical results of the preceding sections are the aggregated demands of a large number of individuals. As Herman Wold points out, the "Slutsky condition" has no direct analogue for aggregated market demands unless very rigid assumptions are employed.[1] It can, however, be shown that the simpler "Hotelling condition" has the property that, if it is satisfied for all individuals, it will also be satisfied for the market as a whole.[2] It is therefore possible to test the hypothesis that the Hotelling symmetry condition holds for the appropriate coefficients of the demand functions for liquid assets, by assuming that r_0 is constant. If r_0 is constant, then

$$(3.15) \qquad \frac{\partial x_i}{\partial r_j} = \frac{\partial x_j}{\partial (r_0 - r_j)} \frac{\partial (r_0 - r_j)}{\partial r_j} = -\frac{\partial x_i}{\partial (r_0 - r_j)},$$

and

$$(3.16) \qquad \frac{\partial x_i}{\partial r_j} = \frac{\partial x_j}{\partial r_i}.$$

Letting q_{ij} denote $\partial x_i/\partial r_j$, the "Hotelling condition" as applied to the preceding estimates suggests the following linear restrictions on the coefficients of the regression system described in (3.9):

$$q_{dt} = q_{td}$$

$$(3.17) \qquad q_{d\bar{s}} = q_{\bar{s}d}$$

$$q_{t\bar{s}} = q_{\bar{s}t}.$$

The test of the "Hotelling condition" is simply a test of a general linear hypothesis involving the β vector, and may be described by

$$(3.18) \qquad C\beta = 0,$$

where C is an arbitrary matrix and β is the coefficient vector described in (3.9).

We wish to test the hypothesis that particular elements of the β vector are equal. The relevant elements are the corresponding cross price terms. We wish particularly to test the hypothesis that the effect

---

[1] Herman Wold, *Demand Analysis* (New York: John Wiley & Sons, Inc., 1953), chap. 7.

[2] See Henry Schultz, *The Theory and Measurement of Demand* (Chicago: University of Chicago Press, 1938), chap. **XIX**, 628–35.

of a change in the price of the ith asset on the demand for the jth asset is equal to the effect of a change in the price of the jth asset on the demand for the ith asset. The C matrix will be $w \times MJ$, where w denotes the number of restrictions on the coefficients. A row of the C matrix will contain zeros, a one, and a minus one as elements. Each row will then select the appropriate coefficients in the β vector and impose the equality restriction.

For testing the linear hypothesis, (3.17), we utilize the following F-statistic described by S. N. Roy:[1]

(3.19)
$$F_{w,(n-m)} = \frac{n-m}{w} \frac{y'\Sigma^{-1}X(X'\Sigma^{-1}X)^{-1}C'[C(X'\Sigma^{-1}X)^{-1}C']^{-1}C(X'\Sigma^{-1}X)^{-1}X'\Sigma^{-1}y}{y'\Sigma^{-1}y - y'\Sigma^{-1}X(X'\Sigma^{-1}X)^{-1}X'\Sigma^{-1}y}$$

with $n = MS$, the number of observations, $m = MJ$, the number of independent variables in the entire set of equations, and w = number of restrictions implied by the hypothesis. As Σ is generally unknown, it is replaced by an estimate of the disturbance variance-covariance matrix formed from the single equation least squares residuals.

The test was applied to each equation set in the eleven years, with the result that for all years it was not possible to reject the hypothesis that the "Hotelling conditions" were satisfied. This test lends much credence to the belief that the traditional theory of consumer behavior can be applied to the theory of the demand for financial assets.

Theil and Goldberger have demonstrated the desirability of including relevant a priori information in the estimation procedure.[2] It is possible to estimate (3.9) in light of the "Hotelling condition" restrictions (3.17). In order to include the "Hotelling conditions" in the estimation procedure, it is necessary to minimize

(3.20) $$(y - X\beta)' \Sigma^{-1} (y - X\beta) - \mu'(R\beta - r)$$

with respect to the elements of β, where y, X, and β are as defined in Eq. (3.9), μ' is a vector of Lagrange multipliers, R is a matrix, and r is a vector, together defining the restrictions. The estimation obtained from this minimization will satisfy the condition that

(3.21) $$R\hat{\beta} = r.$$

---

[1] S. N. Roy, *Some Aspects of Multivariate Analysis* (New York: John Wiley & Sons, Inc., 1957).

[2] H. Theil and A. S. Goldberger, "On Pure and Mixed Statistical Estimation in Economics," *International Economic Review*, **II** (1960).

Given the particular restrictions implied by (3.17), R is simply equal to the C matrix defined in (3.18), and r is a zero vector.

The restricted efficient estimates of the coefficients of the demand functions for demand deposits, time deposits, and savings and loan association shares are listed in Tables 14, 15, and 16 respectively. The restricted efficient estimates differ from the efficient and single equation least squares estimates owing to the gain in efficiency resulting from the addition of restrictions on the coefficient estimates. A summary of own price and cross substitution coefficients is listed in Table 17, and a summary of income, own price, and cross elasticities is included in Table 18.

The results of the restricted efficient cross-section regressions may be summarized as follows:

1. The income coefficients for all the assets are significantly positive, implying that each of the assets is a "superior" asset.[1] The income elasticity for demand deposits is approximately unity in all years. The income elasticity of time deposits is greater than the income elasticity of demand deposits in the early years; the time deposit income elasticity, however, falls sharply in the later years of the analysis. The savings and loan association shares have an income elasticity which is lower than that of demand deposits and time deposits.

2. The own price coefficients of demand deposits and time deposits are highly significant; the demand for savings and loan association shares, however, seems to be quite insensitive to changes in the rate of return on these shares.

3. Demand deposits and time deposits appear to be very weak substitutes in the early years of the analysis. In nine out of the eleven cross sections, the cross substitution effect between demand deposits and time deposits implies independence in demand.

4. The liabilities of savings and loan associations and demand deposits in commercial banks appear to be independent in demand. The cross substitution coefficient between demand deposits and savings and loan association shares does not significantly differ from zero in any of the eleven years. The relatively high standard errors of the cross substitution terms cannot be explained by

---

[1] The traditional tests of significance employed in this section must be regarded with some caution since they do not take explicit account of pre-testing.

arguing that the interest rates are highly collinear. Indeed, the simple correlations among interest rates are very small. Moreover, if multicollinearity was a serious problem, one would not expect to find significant coefficients for the own price terms. The significance of the own price terms, in addition to the low degree of multicollinearity as measured by the simple correlation coefficients among interest rates, lends support to the interpretation that the liabilities of the non-bank financial intermediaries under study are not close substitutes for demand deposits.

5. Demand deposits and mutual savings bank deposits appear to be short-run complements and long-run substitutes. The complementary relationship lends support to the Tobin-Brainard hypothesis that complementarity relationships may exist whenever the public and financial intermediaries hold the same assets.

6. The substitution coefficients between time deposits and savings and loan association shares do not significantly differ from zero in any of the eleven cross-section regressions. The implication of this finding is that time deposits and savings and loan association shares are independent in demand.

7. Time deposits and mutual savings bank deposits appear to be short-run substitutes. The substitution relationship is, however, quite weak in the later-year regressions. The coefficients of the mutual savings bank dummy variable are positive in the early years of the analysis, implying a long-run complementarity relationship between the two assets. In the later years, both the coefficients of the dummy variable and the substitution coefficients imply that time deposits and mutual savings deposits are independent in demand.

8. Savings and loan association shares appear to be weak substitutes for mutual savings bank deposits in the short run. The coefficients of the mutual savings bank dummy variable imply a weak long-run complementarity relationship.

It was shown in Chapter 2 that the substitution relationships between money, as it is narrowly defined, and other liquid assets play a crucial role in determining the effectiveness of monetary policy. One of the necessary conditions for a loss in the effectiveness of monetary policy due to financial intermediation is a strong substitution relationship between money and other financial assets. The results of the restricted efficient estimation procedure tend to reject the hypothesis that time deposits, savings and loan association shares, and mutual savings bank deposits are close substitutes for demand deposits.

Testing the Stability of the Demand Functions Over Time

The discussion of the effectiveness of monetary policy underscored the importance of the stability of the demand function for money as a key determinant of the potential effectiveness of any monetary action. The tests of the stability hypothesis based on the single equation least squares estimates indicated that it was not possible to reject the hypothesis that the demand functions for demand deposits, time deposits, and savings and loan association shares were stable over the time period 1949–59.

It was not possible to compute a pooled regression for the restricted efficient estimates over the entire time period, nor was it possible to test the stability hypothesis directly from the restricted efficient estimates owing to capacity limitations on the computer program. Pooled regressions of the restricted efficient estimates were, however, computed for the periods 1949–53 and 1954–58. These pooled regressions are listed in Table 19 and a matrix of own price, cross, and income elasticities for each of the pooled regressions is listed in Table 2.

TABLE 2. MATRIX OF OWN PRICE, CROSS, AND INCOME ELASTICITIES
Pooled Restricted Efficient Estimates

Dependent variable	Elasticity Estimates at the Mean				
	η_{xd}	η_{xt}	η_{xs}	η_{xm}	η_{xy}
1949–53					
Demand deposits	−.32	.21	−.01	−.13	.98
Time deposits	.12	−.54	.05	.61	.95
Savings and loan association shares	−.01	.02	−.01	.18	.63
1954–58					
Demand deposits	−.38	−.06	.19	−.17	.94
Time deposits	−.03	−.81	−.11	.39	.49
Savings and loan association shares	.06	−.09	.12	.22	.59

Although it was not possible to reject the stability hypothesis, a review of the coefficients in the demand functions for individual years suggests that these coefficients have been changing in a remarkably regular fashion. This observation is confirmed by the pooled regression estimates. One observes, for example, a gradual decline in the income coefficients of both demand deposits and time deposits, and a corresponding increase in the income coefficient of savings and loan association shares. Moreover, the own price and cross price terms reflect similar regular patterns of change. This is particularly true of the savings and loan association shares own price coefficient and of the cross substitution coefficients between demand deposits and time deposits, demand deposits and savings and loan association shares, and time deposits and savings and loan association shares. Demand deposits and time deposits appear to have become poorer substitutes in the postwar period, whereas demand deposits and savings and loan association shares seem to have become better substitutes.

The theory of consumer behavior described in Chapter 2 suggested that the coefficients of the demand functions for any asset could in principle be affected by changes in the quality of other assets. There is evidence that there were quality changes in the characteristics of the liabilities of savings and loan associations. The 1950 revision of the Federal Savings and Loan Insurance Corporation insurance regulations, which increased insurance coverage on savings and loan association shares to $10,000, presumably changed the quality of these assets in the direction of making savings and loan association shares more comparable to demand deposits and time deposits.

It is interesting to note that in 1951 and 1952 the cross substitution coefficients between demand deposits and savings and loan association shares, and time deposits and savings and loan association shares changed signs. In the period before the change in insurance provisions, the cross substitution terms implied a non-significant complementary relationship between demand deposits and savings and loan association shares and time deposits and savings and loan association shares. In the period following the change in insurance provisions, the signs of the cross substitution terms imply substitution relationships. Whether quality changes caused the observed changes in the estimated coefficients cannot be unambiguously determined. What is clear, however, is that the observed changes in the coefficients are not statistically significant and therefore one must reject the hypothesis that quality changes have had substantial effects on the stability of the parameters of the demand functions.

As a final test of the stability hypothesis, the parameter estimates of the demand functions during periods of "easy" monetary policy were compared with estimates of the demand function parameters during periods of "tight" monetary policy.

Gurley and Shaw have suggested that periods of monetary stringency could induce financial innovations which would have the effect of reducing the stability of the demand for money. This hypothesis can be investigated by comparing pooled regressions for years of monetary ease with pooled regressions for years of monetary stringency. The years 1954 and 1958 were selected to represent years of relative monetary ease and the years 1956, 1957, and 1959 were selected to represent years of relative monetary stringency. The estimated coefficients and their standard errors are listed in Table 3.

TABLE 3. MATRIX OF OWN PRICE, CROSS AND INCOME COEFFICIENTS

Pooled Restricted Efficient Estimates

Dependent variable	Independent Variables				
	P_d	P_t	P_s	P_m	Y
	"Easy" Money Period 1954, 1958				
Demand deposits	−498	−9	33	−78	.364
	(105)	(28)	(28)	(42)	(.044)
Time deposits	−9	−93	10	81	.084
	(28)	(18)	(11)	(35)	(.036)
Savings and loan association shares	33	10	−24	22	.069
	(28)	(11)	(15)	(18)	(.020)
	"Tight" Money Period 1956, 1957, 1959				
Demand deposits	−494	1	31	−93	.345
	(80)	(23)	(25)	(34)	(.033)
Time deposits	1	−101	4	67	.092
	(23)	(18)	(12)	(31)	(.029)
Savings and loan association shares	31	4	−28	52	.078
	(25)	(12)	(17)	(17)	(.017)

Inspection of Table 3 reveals that the coefficients of the demand functions estimated during periods of relative monetary ease do not significantly differ from the corresponding coefficients estimated during periods of monetary stringency. The results of this test are consistent with the following alternative hypotheses:

1. That monetary stringency does not induce financial innovation.

2. That induced financial innovation has no significant effect on the parameters of the demand functions for liquid assets.

Regardless of which hypothesis is correct, the results clearly indicate that the demand functions for demand deposits, time deposits, and savings and loan association shares have exhibited remarkable stability over periods of monetary ease and periods of monetary stringency, implying that monetary policy effectiveness has not been reduced as a result of an unstable demand function for money.

CHAPTER 4

Conclusions

The results summarized in this study have implications for monetary theory, the conduct and effectiveness of monetary policy, and the general question of monetary controls.

Recent monetary theory has placed much emphasis on the role of financial intermediaries in the monetary process. The attention focused on these intermediaries is based on the belief that the liabilities of financial intermediaries are close substitutes for money. The empirical results presented in this study cast substantial doubt on this widely held assumption. Indeed, during the postwar period, when financial intermediary liabilities grew at an extraordinary rate, it was impossible to reject the hypothesis that the demand for money was independent of changes in the yields on the liabilities of financial intermediaries. In particular, the evidence supports the view that the demand for demand deposits was not significantly affected by changes in the yields on time deposits, savings and loan association shares, and mutual savings bank deposits. Since data limitations precluded the explicit estimation of demand functions for currency holdings, one cannot rule out the possibility that the liabilities of financial intermediaries are substitutes for currency. There is, however, no independent evidence to support this hypothesis and it deserves further investigation.

Since demand deposits do not appear to be close substitutes for other liquid assets, the investigation undertaken here suggests that a narrow definition of money be employed in further empirical studies. Utilizing the narrow definition of money avoids many of the conceptual problems of interpreting interest rate and income effects which will vary according to the definition of money adopted. The variety of definitions of

43

money employed in previous empirical studies has unfortunately con-
founded the economist's knowledge of the relevant parameters of the
demand function, and this confusion can be avoided by a stricter ad-
herence to a single definition. Adoption of a narrow definition of money
need not preclude an analysis of the effects of other liquid assets on the
monetary mechanism; these assets, however, should be introduced into
a monetary model by means other than defining money more broadly.

The findings of the study cast doubt on the assertion that the growth
of financial intermediaries has substantially reduced the effectiveness
of monetary policy. The evidence does not support the view that the
demand function for money has become less stable, nor does the evidence
support the view that the demand for money and the supply of money
are interdependent as a result of induced financial innovation. The
results do, however, suggest that changes in the quality of financial
assets may affect the parameters of the demand function for money.
Although the evidence does not establish the proposition that quality
changes have had substantial effects, the question deserves further investigation at both the theoretical and empirical level.

The suggestion of extending monetary controls to non-bank financial
intermediaries has already provoked a host of criticisms. The evidence
presented in this paper strongly suggests that further extension of
monetary controls be held in abeyance until such time when there exists
more empirical support for the necessity of such controls. The implication of the analysis is that the effectiveness of monetary policy has not
been impaired as a result of financial intermediation, and the findings
lend no support to the proposed policies which seek to extend monetary
controls to non-bank financial intermediaries.

APPENDIX A

Demand Function Estimates

Demand Deposits, Time Deposits,
Savings and Loan Association Shares

TABLE 4. DEMAND DEPOSITS—DEMAND FUNCTIONS

Single Equation Least Squares Estimates

1949–59

Year	Y	r_d	r_t	r_s	r_m	D_m	I	Cal	DC	Ill	NY	W	S	C	NE	R^2
1949	.475 (.095)	642 (204)	−147 (84)	23 (39)	144 (80)	−319 (138)	464 (233)	50 (274)	150 (264)	200 (238)	751 (217)	66 (217)	−20 (205)	85 (216)	57 (238)	.902
1950	.483 (.096)	641 (225)	−154 (85)	53 (45)	203 (106)	−425 (187)	452 (249)	−5 (304)	136 (296)	141 (250)	705 (225)	12 (240)	−84 (222)	20 (232)	−16 (251)	.902
1951	.476 (.079)	628 (217)	−65 (79)	72 (51)	181 (106)	−414 (195)	441 (250)	−148 (305)	79 (292)	20 (240)	613 (219)	−122 (235)	−220 (221)	−111 (224)	−170 (242)	.906
1952	.454 (.094)	660 (231)	−19 (64)	47 (49)	97 (86)	−281 (172)	415 (257)	−107 (314)	124 (300)	65 (259)	628 (239)	−91 (252)	−181 (225)	−65 (237)	−144 (253)	.887
1953	.411 (.095)	629 (202)	−28 (64)	46 (58)	154 (81)	−411 (170)	454 (250)	−85 (363)	166 (337)	103 (301)	638 (278)	−72 (294)	−156 (268)	−25 (278)	−121 (292)	.883
1954	.399 (.086)	639 (188)	3 (71)	26 (58)	145 (82)	−379 (176)	480 (256)	11 (362)	260 (343)	140 (299)	644 (279)	−18 (300)	−124 (274)	−10 (278)	−109 (290)	.882
1955	.407 (.082)	703 (184)	3 (73)	23 (61)	186 (87)	−466 (192)	568 (259)	8 (371)	249 (351)	124 (304)	593 (286)	−36 (311)	−128 (285)	−29 (289)	−134 (299)	.880
1956	.364 (.075)	559 (177)	−34 (80)	44 (79)	150 (79)	−413 (184)	468 (256)	31 (443)	296 (411)	158 (369)	651 (362)	16 (378)	−85 (356)	16 (351)	−82 (372)	.877
1957	.338 (.069)	594 (175)	59 (70)	37 (69)	146 (74)	−430 (191)	371 (246)	−76 (387)	249 (343)	53 (305)	536 (306)	−64 (314)	−188 (300)	−58 (290)	−166 (306)	.889
1958	.302 (.075)	566 (175)	36 (73)	−42 (62)	156 (76)	−478 (206)	272 (266)	417 (412)	735 (366)	452 (332)	900 (330)	354 (343)	221 (320)	327 (315)	218 (330)	.878
1959	.331 (.067)	581 (154)	72 (71)	14 (79)	105 (63)	−354 (180)	271 (234)	40 (420)	386 (385)	74 (349)	543 (344)	26 (361)	−94 (344)	−8 (338)	−88 (345)	.897

TABLE 5. TIME DEPOSITS—DEMAND FUNCTIONS

Single Equation Least Squares Estimates

1949-59

Year	Y	r_d	r_t	r_s	r_m	D_m	Cal	DC	Ill	NY	W	S	C	NE	R^2
1949	.203 (.058)	−127 (125)	194 (51)	11 (24)	−224 (50)	444 (85)	−81 (162)	−287 (158)	−158 (144)	−240 (130)	−292 (126)	−316 (118)	−287 (124)	−284 (138)	.842
1950	.232 (.055)	−111 (129)	216 (48)	9 (25)	−271 (61)	527 (107)	−160 (170)	−355 (167)	−220 (142)	−293 (126)	−362 (132)	−366 (121)	−339 (126)	−326 (137)	.843
1951	.195 (.051)	−65 (140)	124 (50)	−20 (32)	−290 (69)	575 (126)	68 (188)	−162 (182)	−26 (150)	−139 (136)	−157 (141)	−169 (131)	−144 (133)	−67 (144)	.820
1952	.191 (.062)	−227 (153)	92 (42)	−42 (32)	−194 (57)	436 (115)	120 (202)	−112 (195)	44 (169)	−47 (154)	−114 (159)	−109 (140)	−92 (148)	−41 (158)	.792
1953	.187 (.064)	−158 (136)	86 (43)	−50 (39)	−188 (54)	436 (114)	176 (236)	−57 (219)	95 (198)	−19 (181)	−56 (188)	−72 (169)	−41 (176)	1 (184)	.788
1954	.156 (.060)	−158 (132)	79 (50)	−52 (41)	−173 (58)	417 (124)	241 (245)	2 (232)	165 (204)	55 (190)	5 (200)	−30 (180)	8 (183)	55 (190)	.764
1955	.147 (.059)	−136 (132)	89 (52)	−43 (44)	−161 (62)	405 (137)	225 (253)	2 (240)	144 (210)	44 (197)	−20 (209)	−55 (189)	−14 (192)	25 (197)	.746
1956	.133 (.056)	−118 (133)	122 (59)	−76 (59)	−140 (59)	380 (138)	279 (313)	83 (291)	207 (264)	73 (258)	28 (264)	−17 (246)	43 (242)	57 (255)	.738
1957	.137 (.060)	−61 (154)	139 (61)	−15 (61)	−54 (65)	199 (168)	−32 (317)	−177 (280)	−22 (254)	−200 (253)	−231 (252)	−279 (238)	−170 (30)	−242 (240)	.692
1958	.121 (.069)	−5 (165)	201 (68)	−50 (58)	−46 (72)	183 (194)	56 (348)	−73 (308)	43 (287)	−164 (283)	−191 (283)	−269 (258)	−143 (255)	−212 (264)	.676
1959	.112 (.080)	−89 (186)	134 (85)	−49 (95)	−66 (77)	230 (219)	184 (467)	−8 (429)	122 (396)	−8 (388)	−62 (396)	−143 (376)	−35 (367)	−77 (371)	.592

47

TABLE 6. SAVINGS AND LOAN ASSOCIATION SHARES—DEMAND FUNCTIONS

Single Equation Least Squares Estimates

1949–59

Year	Y	r_d	r_l	r_s	r_m	A	D_m	Cal	DC	Ill	NY	W	S	C	NE	R^2
1949	.042	1	−8	−1	−33	.499	75	−37	118	−32	−41	−24	3	−13	−16	.915
	(.021)	(45)	(19)	(10)	(18)	(.084)	(31)	(63)	(67)	(56)	(47)	(48)	(45)	(46)	(51)	
1950	.042	−35	−4	5	−47	.557	99	−97	73	−79	−62	−62	−34	−45	−45	.928
	(.020)	(48)	(18)	(11)	(23)	(.082)	(39)	(74)	(80)	(63)	(49)	(55)	(50)	(52)	(55)	
1951	.045	−71	−8	8	−61	.501	128	−115	125	−81	−71	−75	−46	−59	−55	.934
	(.019)	(54)	(19)	(14)	(26)	(.070)	(47)	(80)	(84)	(65)	(53)	(57)	(54)	(54)	(57)	
1952	.053	−86	0	11	−55	.499	126	−161	97	−122	0	−1	−0	0	0	.933
	(.024)	(59)	(16)	(13)	(22)	(.063)	(44)	(86)	(89)	(73)	(61)	(64)	(58)	(61)	(63)	
1953	.057	−77	−11	22	−46	.469	116	−166	57	−149	−105	−124	−94	−104	−109	.913
	(.030)	(65)	(20)	(20)	(26)	(.064)	(54)	(119)	(120)	(103)	(88)	(92)	(84)	(87)	(90)	
1954	.042	−90	−37	9	−33	.548	102	−104	123	−95	−17	−33	−6	−27	−29	.937
	(.027)	(58)	(22)	(18)	(26)	(.058)	(55)	(110)	(110)	(94)	(84)	(89)	(80)	(81)	(84)	
1955	.068	−106	−17	52	−65	.513	186	−330	−6	−246	−189	−245	−190	−218	−223	.972
	(.030)	(64)	(21)	(16)	(31)	(.052)	(69)	(100)	(96)	(81)	(70)	(75)	(61)	(66)	(69)	
1956	.075	−137	−30	−30	−82	.452	237	−279	142	−171	−118	−164	−110	−160	−150	.924
	(.033)	(77)	(35)	(35)	(35)	(.049)	(80)	(184)	(173)	(156)	(150)	(153)	(143)	(141)	(148)	
1957	.068	−101	−25	13	−80	.478	253	−230	148	−122	−60	−100	−47	−99	−93	.945
	(.031)	(77)	(31)	(30)	(32)	(.048)	(84)	(157)	(141)	(126)	(128)	(126)	(119)	(114)	(121)	
1958	.084	−116	−25	51	−75	.441	250	−334	121	−232	−195	−254	−181	−220	−236	.939
	(.037)	(85)	(35)	(30)	(37)	(.049)	(99)	(178)	(161)	(148)	(145)	(145)	(133)	(130)	(136)	
1959	.103	−81	2	47	−77	.420	269	−423	148	−289	−299	−328	−248	−286	−309	.937
	(.042)	(98)	(43)	(49)	(40)	(.049)	(112)	(238)	(221)	(203)	(198)	(202)	(192)	(187)	(190)	

48

TABLE 7. MATRIX OF OWN PRICE AND CROSS SUBSTITUTION TERMS

Single Equation Least Squares Estimates

1949–59

Year	Dependent Variable	Independent Variables			
		P_d	P_t	P_s	P_m
1949	D	−642 (204)	147 (84)	−23 (39)	−144 (80)
	T	127 (125)	−194 (51)	−11 (24)	224 (50)
	S	−1 (45)	8 (19)	1 (10)	33 (18)
1950	D	−641 (225)	154 (85)	−53 (45)	−203 (106)
	T	111 (129)	−216 (48)	−9 (25)	271 (61)
	S	35 (48)	4 (18)	−5 (11)	47 (23)
1951	D	−628 (217)	65 (79)	−72 (51)	−181 (106)
	T	65 (140)	−124 (50)	20 (32)	290 (69)
	S	71 (54)	8 (19)	−8 (14)	61 (26)
1952	D	−660 (231)	19 (64)	−47 (49)	−97 (86)
	T	227 (153)	−92 (42)	42 (32)	194 (57)
	S	86 (59)	0 (16)	−11 (13)	55 (22)
1953	D	−629 (202)	28 (64)	−46 (58)	−154 (81)
	T	158 (136)	−86 (43)	50 (39)	188 (54)
	S	77 (65)	11 (20)	−22 (20)	46 (26)
1954	D	−639 (188)	−3 (71)	−26 (58)	−145 (82)
	T	158 (132)	−79 (50)	52 (41)	173 (58)
	S	90 (58)	37 (22)	−9 (18)	33 (26)

TABLE 7. MATRIX OF OWN PRICE AND CROSS SUBSTITUTION TERMS—(*cont.*)

Single Equation Least Squares Estimates

1949–59

Year	Dependent Variable	Independent Variables			
		P_d	P_t	P_s	P_m
1955	D	−703 (184)	−3 (73)	−23 (61)	−186 (87)
	T	136 (132)	−89 (52)	43 (44)	161 (62)
	S	106 (64)	17 (21)	−52 (16)	65 (31)
1956	D	−559 (177)	34 (80)	−44 (79)	−150 (79)
	T	118 (133)	−122 (59)	76 (59)	140 (59)
	S	137 (77)	30 (35)	−30 (35)	82 (35)
1957	D	−594 (175)	−59 (70)	−37 (69)	−146 (74)
	T	61 (154)	−139 (61)	15 (61)	54 (65)
	S	101 (77)	25 (31)	−13 (30)	80 (32)
1958	D	−566 (175)	−36 (73)	−42 (62)	−156 (76)
	T	−5 (165)	−201 (68)	50 (58)	46 (72)
	S	116 (85)	25 (35)	−51 (30)	75 (37)
1959	D	−581 (154)	−72 (71)	−14 (79)	−105 (63)
	T	89 (186)	−134 (85)	49 (95)	66 (77)
	S	81 (98)	2 (43)	−47 (49)	77 (40)

TABLE 8. MATRIX OF OWN PRICE, CROSS, AND INCOME ELASTICITIES

Single Equation Least Squares Estimates

1949–59

Year	Dependent Variable	Elasticity Estimates at the Mean				
		η_{xd}	η_{xt}	η_{xs}	η_{xm}	η_{xy}
1949	D	− .32	.31	− .13	− .19	1.08
	T	.15	− .96	− .15	.70	1.13
	S	.00	.12	.03	.30	.66
1950	D	− .31	.31	− .28	− .26	1.07
	T	.14	−1.12	− .12	.90	1.34
	S	.11	.06	− .19	.40	.63
1951	D	− .29	.13	− .36	− .23	1.08
	T	.08	− .66	.27	.97	1.16
	S	.20	.10	− .26	.48	.63
1952	D	− .28	.15	− .37	− .25	1.13
	T	.26	− .52	.55	.68	1.14
	S	.21	.00	− .30	.41	.67
1953	D	− .32	.07	− .25	− .22	1.03
	T	.19	− .51	.65	.66	1.11
	S	.17	.12	− .54	.31	.64
1954	D	− .35	− .01	− .14	− .22	1.00
	T	.20	− .48	.66	.60	.90
	S	.19	.38	− .18	.19	.41
1955	D	− .39	− .01	− .12	− .28	1.03
	T	.18	− .55	.54	.57	.86
	S	.14	.17	−1.01	.30	.52
1956	D	− .34	.10	− .24	− .24	.95
	T	.16	− .82	.94	.51	.79
	S	.25	.27	− .47	.40	.60
1957	D	− .43	− .23	− .22	− .26	.94
	T	.09	−1.09	.18	.19	.77
	S	.19	.26	− .21	.38	.51
1958	D	− .42	− .14	.25	− .28	.84
	T	− .01	−1.53	.57	.16	.63
	S	.21	.25	− .76	.33	.58
1959	D	− .46	− .31	− .09	− .20	.96
	T	.13	−1.04	.56	.22	.59
	S	.14	− .02	− .65	.32	.66

TABLE 9. DEMAND DEPOSITS—DEMAND FUNCTIONS

Efficient Estimates

1949–59

Year	Y	r_d	r_t	r_s	r_m	D_m	I	Cal	DC	Ill	NY	W	S	C	NE
1949	.476	644	−146	22	144	−318	483	43	144	196	746	59	−27	78	50
	(.095)	(204)	(84)	(39)	(80)	(138)	(222)	(272)	(263)	(238)	(216)	(216)	(204)	(214)	(237)
1950	.482	638	−155	55	204	−429	401	9	148	151	714	26	−70	35	−1
	(.096)	(225)	(85)	(45)	(106)	(187)	(236)	(303)	(296)	(250)	(224)	(239)	(221)	(231)	(250)
1951	.475	625	−67	73	181	−416	401	−133	91	30	623	−108	−206	−97	−155
	(.079)	(217)	(79)	(51)	(106)	(195)	(240)	(304)	(291)	(239)	(218)	(234)	(219)	(223)	(241)
1952	.453	657	−21	48	96	−282	387	−98	131	71	634	−82	−172	−56	−134
	(.094)	(231)	(64)	(49)	(86)	(172)	(241)	(313)	(300)	(259)	(238)	(250)	(223)	(236)	(251)
1953	.411	629	−28	46	154	−411	461	−88	163	101	636	−74	−159	−28	−124
	(.095)	(202)	(64)	(58)	(81)	(170)	(244)	(363)	(336)	(301)	(278)	(293)	(268)	(277)	(291)
1954	.399	639	3	26	145	−379	492	7	256	137	641	−23	−128	−15	−113
	(.086)	(188)	(71)	(58)	(82)	(176)	(249)	(362)	(342)	(298)	(279)	(299)	(273)	(277)	(289)
1955	.411	714	13	32	183	−458	592	−50	193	76	545	−89	−180	−80	−186
	(.082)	(184)	(72)	(61)	(87)	(192)	(253)	(369)	(349)	(302)	(284)	(309)	(283)	(287)	(296)
1956	.367	558	−31	46	151	−414	538	−11	258	127	619	−23	−124	−22	−124
	(.075)	(177)	(80)	(79)	(79)	(184)	(249)	(442)	(410)	(368)	(361)	(376)	(355)	(350)	(370)
1957	.344	591	64	37	147	−430	490	−147	185	3	484	−128	−252	−121	−234
	(.069)	(175)	(70)	(69)	(74)	(191)	(234)	(385)	(341)	(303)	(304)	(311)	(297)	(288)	(303)
1958	.311	559	43	−39	157	−476	428	310	639	374	820	257	126	233	117
	(.075)	(175)	(73)	(62)	(76)	(206)	(255)	(408)	(362)	(330)	(327)	(339)	(316)	(311)	(326)
1959	.336	576	77	17	106	−353	370	−32	321	21	488	−40	−159	−72	−156
	(.067)	(154)	(70)	(79)	(63)	(180)	(229)	(418)	(383)	(348)	(343)	(359)	(342)	(336)	(343)

TABLE 10. TIME DEPOSITS—DEMAND FUNCTIONS

Efficient Estimates

1949–59

Year	z	r_3	r_t	r_s	r_m	D_m	Cal	DC	Ill	NY	W	S	C	NE
1949	.208 (.058)	-127 (126)	194 (51)	11 (24)	-224 (50)	444 (85)	-81 (162)	-287 (158)	-158 (144)	-240 (130)	-292 (126)	-316 (118)	-287 (124)	-284 (138)
1950	.232 (.055)	-111 (129)	216 (48)	9 (25)	-271 (61)	527 (107)	-160 (170)	-355 (167)	-220 (142)	-293 (126)	-362 (132)	-366 (121)	-339 (126)	-326 (137)
1951	.195 (.051)	-65 (140)	124 (50)	-20 (32)	-290 (69)	575 (126)	68 (188)	-162 (182)	-26 (150)	-139 (136)	-157 (140)	-169 (131)	-144 (133)	-67 (144)
1952	.190 (.062)	-227 (153)	92 (42)	-42 (32)	-194 (57)	436 (115)	120 (202)	-121 (195)	44 (169)	-47 (154)	-114 (159)	-109 (140)	-92 (148)	-41 (158)
1953	.187 (.064)	-158 (136)	86 (43)	-50 (39)	-188 (54)	436 (114)	176 (236)	-57 (219)	95 (198)	-19 (181)	-56 (188)	-72 (169)	-41 (176)	1 (184)
1954	.156 (.060)	-158 (132)	79 (50)	-52 (41)	-173 (58)	417 (124)	241 (245)	7 (232)	165 (204)	55 (190)	5 (200)	-30 (180)	8 (183)	55 (190)
1955	.141 (.058)	-154 (131)	74 (51)	-57 (43)	-156 (62)	392 (137)	298 (248)	78 (235)	206 (206)	106 (193)	46 (205)	-1 (184)	48 (187)	88 (192)
1956	.133 (.056)	-118 (133)	122 (59)	-76 (59)	-140 (59)	380 (138)	279 (313)	83 (291)	207 (264)	73 (258)	28 (264)	-17 (246)	43 (242)	57 (255)
1957	.137 (.060)	-61 (154)	139 (61)	-15 (61)	-54 (65)	199 (168)	-32 (317)	-177 (280)	-22 (254)	-200 (253)	-231 (252)	-279 (238)	-170 (230)	-242 (240)
1958	.121 (.069)	-5 (165)	201 (68)	-50 (58)	-46 (72)	183 (194)	56 (348)	-73 (308)	43 (287)	-164 (283)	-191 (283)	-269 (260)	-143 (255)	-212 (264)
1959	.112 (.080)	-89 (186)	134 (85)	-49 (95)	-66 (77)	230 (219)	184 (467)	-8 (429)	122 (396)	-8 (388)	-62 (396)	-142 (376)	-35 (367)	-77 (371)

53

TABLE 11. SAVINGS AND LOAN ASSOCIATION SHARES—DEMAND FUNCTIONS

Efficient Estimates

1949–59

Year	Y	r_d	r_t	r_s	r_m	A	D_m	Cal	DC	Ill	NY	W	S	C	NE
1949	.043	1	−8	−2	−33	.479	76	−31	126	−27	−39	−20	1	−10	−13
	(.021)	(45)	(19)	(10)	(18)	(.078)	(31)	(62)	(65)	(56)	(47)	(47)	(45)	(46)	(51)
1950	.042	−34	−4	5	−47	.553	99	−95	76	−78	−61	−61	−33	−43	−44
	(.020)	(48)	(18)	(11)	(23)	(.079)	(39)	(73)	(78)	(62)	(49)	(54)	(50)	(51)	(54)
1951	.045	−67	−8	6	−61	.478	130	−102	141	−70	−66	−68	−38	−52	−49
	(.019)	(53)	(19)	(13)	(26)	(.065)	(47)	(79)	(82)	(64)	(52)	(57)	(53)	(53)	(56)
1952	.054	−83	1	9	−55	.475	128	−147	115	−109	−74	−98	−64	−81	−78
	(.024)	(59)	(16)	(13)	(22)	(.059)	(44)	(85)	(87)	(72)	(61)	(64)	(57)	(60)	(63)
1953	.058	−76	−10	20	−45	.449	118	−154	75	−136	−100	−117	−86	−97	−104
	(.030)	(65)	(20)	(19)	(26)	(.060)	(54)	(119)	(118)	(102)	(88)	(92)	(84)	(87)	(89)
1954	.044	−90	−36	8	−34	.533	103	−99	134	−88	−18	−32	−4	−25	−29
	(.027)	(58)	(22)	(18)	(26)	(.054)	(55)	(110)	(109)	(93)	(84)	(89)	(80)	(81)	(84)
1955	.070	−104	−15	51	−66	.493	189	−322	8	−238	−190	−242	−188	−216	−222
	(.030)	(64)	(21)	(16)	(31)	(.050)	(69)	(99)	(96)	(81)	(70)	(75)	(61)	(66)	(69)
1956	.077	−138	−29	28	−81	.435	237	−269	155	−162	−113	−162	−108	−157	−151
	(.033)	(77)	(35)	(35)	(35)	(.047)	(80)	(184)	(173)	(156)	(150)	(153)	(143)	(141)	(148)
1957	.072	−104	−22	13	−81	.459	255	−229	157	−119	−70	−108	−53	−103	−102
	(.031)	(77)	(31)	(30)	(32)	(.046)	(84)	(157)	(141)	(126)	(128)	(126)	(119)	(114)	(121)
1958	.088	−122	−24	50	−75	.422	252	−330	134	−224	−201	−258	−183	−222	−242
	(.037)	(85)	(35)	(30)	(37)	(.048)	(99)	(178)	(161)	(148)	(145)	(145)	(133)	(130)	(136)
1959	.107	−90	3	47	−78	.400	274	−418	160	−283	−305	−335	−252	−290	−317
	(.042)	(98)	(43)	(49)	(40)	(.048)	(112)	(238)	(220)	(202)	(198)	(202)	(192)	(187)	(190)

TABLE 12. MATRIX OF OWN PRICE AND CROSS SUBSTITUTION TERMS

Efficient Estimates

1949–59

Year	Dependent Variable	Independent Variables			
		P_d	P_t	P_s	P_m
1949	D	−644	146	−22	−144
		(204)	(84)	(39)	(80)
	T	127	−194	−11	224
		(126)	(51)	(24)	(50)
	S	−1	8	2	33
		(45)	(19)	(10)	(18)
1950	D	−638	155	−55	−204
		(225)	(85)	(45)	(106)
	T	111	−216	9	271
		(129)	(48)	(25)	(61)
	S	34	4	−5	47
		(48)	(18)	(11)	(23)
1951	D	−625	67	−73	−181
		(217)	(79)	(51)	(106)
	T	65	−124	20	290
		(140)	(50)	(32)	(69)
	S	67	8	−6	61
		(53)	(19)	(13)	(26)
1952	D	−657	21	−48	−96
		(231)	(64)	(49)	(86)
	T	227	−92	42	194
		(153)	(42)	(32)	(57)
	S	83	−1	−9	55
		(59)	(16)	(13)	(22)
1953	D	−629	28	−46	−154
		(202)	(64)	(58)	(81)
	T	158	−86	50	188
		(136)	(43)	(39)	(54)
	S	76	10	20	45
		(65)	(20)	(19)	(26)
1954	D	−639	−3	−26	−145
		(188)	(71)	(58)	(82)
	T	158	−79	−52	173
		(132)	(50)	(41)	(58)
	S	90	36	8	34
		(58)	(22)	(18)	(26)

TABLE 12. MATRIX OF OWN PRICE AND CROSS SUBSTITUTION TERMS—(*cont.*)

Efficient Estimates

1949–59

Year	Dependent Variable	Independent Variables			
		P_d	P_t	P_s	P_m
1955	D	−714 (184)	−13 (72)	−32 (61)	−183 (87)
	T	154 (131)	−74 (51)	57 (43)	156 (62)
	S	104 (64)	15 (21)	−51 (16)	66 (31)
1956	D	−558 (177)	31 (80)	−46 (79)	−151 (79)
	T	118 (133)	−122 (59)	76 (59)	140 (59)
	S	138 (77)	29 (35)	−28 (35)	81 (35)
1957	D	−591 (175)	−64 (70)	−37 (69)	−147 (74)
	T	61 (154)	−139 (61)	15 (61)	54 (65)
	S	104 (77)	22 (31)	−13 (30)	81 (32)
1958	D	−559 (175)	−43 (73)	39 (62)	−157 (76)
	T	−5 (165)	−201 (68)	50 (58)	46 (72)
	S	122 (85)	24 (35)	−50 (30)	75 (37)
1959	D	−576 (154)	−77 (70)	−17 (79)	−106 (63)
	T	89 (186)	−134 (85)	49 (95)	66 (77)
	S	90 (98)	3 (43)	−47 (49)	78 (40)

TABLE 13. MATRIX OF OWN PRICE, CROSS, AND INCOME ELASTICITIES

Efficient Estimates

1949–59

Year	Dependent Variable	Elasticity Estimates at the Mean				
		η_{xd}	η_{xt}	η_{xs}	η_{xm}	η_{xy}
1949	D	$-.32$	.30	$-.12$	$-.19$	1.09
	T	.15	$-.96$	$-.15$	.70	1.13
	S	$-.01$	.12	.07	.30	.68
1950	D	$-.31$	.31	$-.29$	$-.26$	1.07
	T	.14	-1.12	$-.12$	.90	1.34
	S	.11	.06	$-.18$	.40	.63
1951	D	$-.29$	.14	$-.37$	$-.23$	1.07
	T	.08	$-.66$	.27	.97	1.16
	S	.19	.09	$-.19$	.48	.63
1952	D	$-.30$	.05	$-.25$	$-.13$	1.07
	T	.26	$-.52$	.55	.68	1.13
	S	.20	$-.01$	$-.22$	.41	.68
1953	D	$-.32$	.07	$-.25$	$-.22$	1.03
	T	.19	$-.51$	.65	.66	1.11
	S	.17	.11	$-.49$	.30	.65
1954	D	$-.35$	$-.01$	$-.14$	$-.22$	1.00
	T	.20	$-.48$	.66	.60	.90
	S	.19	.37	$-.16$	.20	.43
1955	D	$-.40$	$-.03$	$-.17$	$-.28$	1.04
	T	.20	$-.46$	.72	.55	.83
	S	.14	.15	$-.99$	.31	.54
1956	D	$-.34$	.09	$-.25$	$-.24$	.96
	T	.16	$-.82$	.94	.51	.79
	S	.25	.26	$-.44$	.39	.61
1957	D	$-.43$	$-.25$	$-.22$	$-.26$	.96
	T	.09	-1.09	$-.18$	$-.19$	.77
	S	.20	.23	$-.21$	.38	.54
1958	D	$-.42$	$-.17$	.23	$-.28$	.86
	T	$-.01$	-1.53	.57	.16	.63
	S	.22	.24	$-.74$	.33	.60
1959	D	$-.46$	$-.33$	$-.11$	.20	.97
	T	.13	-1.04	.56	.22	.59
	S	.16	$-.03$	$-.04$	.32	.03

TABLE 14. DEMAND DEPOSITS—DEMAND FUNCTIONS

Restricted Efficient Estimates

1949–59

Year	Y	r_d	r_l	r_s	r_m	D_m	I	Cal	DC	Ill	NY	W	S	C	NE
1949	.477	673	−133	17	148	−324	497	46	150	196	744	59	−26	77	49
	(.094)	(181)	(64)	(28)	(76)	(131)	(220)	(240)	(236)	(211)	(196)	(187)	(171)	(185)	(204)
1950	.472	720	−151	17	242	−492	447	144	279	256	798	133	40	139	112
	(.095)	(205)	(67)	(32)	(100)	(176)	(234)	(273)	(270)	(226)	(206)	(213)	(190)	(205)	(220)
1951	.462	693	−83	2	229	−501	432	147	351	243	810	112	27	121	75
	(.079)	(197)	(65)	(35)	(104)	(190)	(238)	(267)	(260)	(212)	(194)	(204)	(183)	(192)	(209)
1952	.439	617	−71	−24	122	−333	413	202	391	322	869	174	92	192	132
	(.094)	(210)	(57)	(36)	(85)	(171)	(239)	(289)	(278)	(240)	(220)	(230)	(198)	(215)	(229)
1953	.367	634	−70	−26	191	−482	463	293	499	415	924	247	151	277	193
	(.093)	(189)	(56)	(41)	(79)	(167)	(243)	(309)	(290)	(259)	(241)	(247)	(220)	(234)	(246)
1954	.361	641	−51	−47	171	−427	500	397	632	464	950	326	205	308	218
	(.084)	(175)	(60)	(39)	(81)	(174)	(249)	(300)	(285)	(249)	(234)	(242)	(214)	(225)	(236)
1955	.376	698	−48	−45	218	−529	589	374	596	423	875	287	178	270	167
	(.081)	(171)	(61)	(42)	(85)	(189)	(253)	(306)	(292)	(253)	(240)	(251)	(225)	(233)	(244)
1956	.335	571	−78	−66	165	−434	498	546	773	590	1064	466	349	433	348
	(.073)	(164)	(65)	(52)	(79)	(184)	(248)	(338)	(310)	(279)	(275)	(278)	(256)	(258)	(277)
1957	.339	589	50	−28	150	−435	472	163	453	246	720	130	9	122	15
	(.069)	(152)	(59)	(48)	(74)	(190)	(233)	(322)	(291)	(257)	(262)	(258)	(242)	(237)	(254)
1958	.302	573	36	−76	165	−494	409	511	813	539	969	429	293	392	275
	(.074)	(153)	(62)	(46)	(76)	(205)	(254)	(357)	(320)	(288)	(293)	(294)	(272)	(270)	(288)
1959	.330	567	59	−37	111	−368	343	251	583	263	722	213	92	168	82
	(.067)	(141)	(63)	(58)	(63)	(180)	(228)	(358)	(330)	(299)	(302)	(305)	(288)	(286)	(296)

TABLE 15. TIME DEPOSITS—DEMAND FUNCTIONS

Restricted Efficient Estimates

1949–59

Year	Y	r_d	r_t	r_s	r_m	D_m	Cal	DC	Ill	NY	W	S	C	NE
1949	.205 (.057)	-133 (64)	182 (46)	2 (13)	-216 (45)	428 (78)	-39 (125)	-250 (124)	-122 (118)	-208 (112)	-256 (95)	-278 (83)	-250 (92)	-243 (104)
1950	.237 (.042)	-151 (67)	206 (44)	7 (14)	-269 (55)	520 (98)	-162 (129)	-361 (128)	-218 (114)	-291 (106)	-361 (98)	-361 (84)	-337 (93)	-323 (101)
1951	.199 (.049)	-83 (65)	129 (45)	-1 (15)	-303 (66)	598 (121)	-9 (138)	-232 (133)	-84 (116)	-190 (108)	-213 (100)	-233 (82)	-204 (90)	-131 (101)
1952	.174 (.060)	-72 (57)	119 (39)	-6 (13)	-195 (55)	445 (112)	50 (152)	-167 (146)	-28 (136)	-127 (128)	-181 (116)	-198 (90)	-164 (105)	-122 (113)
1953	.190 (.060)	-70 (56)	107 (39)	-16 (17)	-201 (52)	468 (110)	57 (158)	-161 (150)	-13 (143)	-125 (138)	-161 (123)	-184 (101)	-146 (114)	-107 (120)
1954	.148 (.057)	-51 (60)	101 (46)	-37 (19)	-171 (57)	422 (122)	223 (168)	-24 (168)	131 (150)	7 (148)	-26 (133)	-72 (111)	-27 (122)	19 (127)
1955	.143 (.057)	-48 (61)	105 (47)	-18 (19)	-163 (60)	414 (134)	161 (177)	-63 (176)	77 (157)	-31 (154)	-84 (143)	-138 (121)	-81 (130)	-42 (136)
1956	.139 (.054)	-78 (65)	144 (53)	-31 (28)	-140 (58)	381 (137)	91 (199)	-98 (191)	41 (177)	-95 (182)	-141 (164)	-187 (145)	-118 (148)	-111 (163)
1957	.127 (.059)	50 (59)	167 (49)	-8 (25)	-44 (64)	185 (168)	-43 (228)	-203 (213)	-47 (188)	-257 (201)	-246 (176)	-317 (159)	-193 (155)	-275 (172)
1958	.120 (.067)	36 (62)	211 (55)	-22 (26)	-49 (71)	194 (193)	-55 (268)	-175 (246)	-61 (225)	-266 (242)	-289 (214)	-375 (192)	-240 (193)	-307 (210)
1959	.097 (.079)	59 (63)	170 (69)	5 (35)	-60 (77)	229 (219)	1 (327)	-199 (308)	-76 (284)	-228 (303)	-236 (268)	-348 (243)	-225 (250)	-261 (263)

TABLE 16. SAVINGS AND LOAN ASSOCIATION SHARES—DEMAND FUNCTIONS

Restricted Efficient Estimates

1949–59

Year	Y	r_d	r_t	r_s	r_m	A	D_m	Cal	DC	Ill	NY	W	S	C	NE
1949	.044 (.020)	17 (28)	2 (13)	-2 (9)	-33 (17)	.478 (.078)	77 (30)	-38 (52)	122 (57)	-35 (48)	-47 (41)	-27 (38)	-7 (36)	-17 (37)	-22 (41)
1950	.036 (.019)	17 (32)	7 (14)	2 (10)	-44 (22)	.544 (.078)	96 (38)	-68 (64)	106 (70)	-60 (56)	-49 (44)	-42 (46)	-18 (43)	-27 (44)	-27 (47)
1951	.036 (.018)	2 (35)	-1 (15)	-2 (13)	-55 (25)	.458 (.064)	123 (47)	-40 (69)	208 (74)	-26 (58)	-33 (47)	-22 (49)	3 (46)	-9 (46)	-5 (49)
1952	.040 (.023)	-24 (36)	-6 (14)	-2 (12)	-46 (21)	.466 (.059)	114 (44)	-59 (74)	197 (77)	-42 (65)	-19 (55)	-26 (55)	-1 (49)	-15 (52)	-10 (54)
1953	.041 (.029)	-26 (41)	-16 (17)	9 (18)	-37 (25)	.448 (.060)	105 (54)	-56 (103)	162 (106)	-61 (92)	-35 (78)	-37 (79)	-15 (73)	-24 (75)	-27 (77)
1954	.033 (.026)	-47 (39)	-37 (19)	-1 (17)	-28 (25)	.535 (.054)	96 (54)	-30 (94)	193 (97)	-39 (83)	24 (74)	24 (74)	44 (67)	24 (69)	22 (71)
1955	.059 (.029)	-45 (42)	-18 (19)	44 (13)	-58 (30)	.500 (.049)	175 (68)	-249 (80)	68 (82)	-190 (71)	-150 (64)	-181 (58)	-138 (46)	-164 (52)	-170 (56)
1956	.062 (.032)	-66 (52)	-31 (28)	11 (33)	-71 (34)	.439 (.047)	222 (80)	-140 (163)	264 (155)	-69 (140)	-35 (132)	-55 (133)	-15 (125)	-63 (124)	-56 (130)
1957	.063 (.030)	-28 (48)	-8 (25)	1 (29)	-73 (32)	.464 (.046)	244 (83)	-158 (146)	205 (134)	-74 (120)	-45 (121)	-50 (116)	-10 (111)	-56 (106)	-57 (113)
1958	.078 (.035)	-76 (46)	-22 (26)	42 (28)	-70 (36)	.430 (.048)	245 (99)	-259 (163)	186 (152)	-177 (140)	161 (136)	-197 (131)	-134 (123)	-173 (120)	-191 (125)
1959	.097 (.041)	-37 (58)	5 (35)	32 (46)	-72 (39)	.411 (.047)	262 (118)	-318 (223)	241 (210)	-211 (194)	-241 (189)	-244 (188)	-174 (180)	-214 (176)	-238 (179)

TABLE 17. MATRIX OF OWN PRICE AND CROSS SUBSTITUTION TERMS

Restricted Efficient Estimates

1949–59

Year	Dependent Variable	Independent Variables			
		P_d	P_t	P_s	P_m
1949	D	−673 (181)	133 (64)	−17 (28)	−148 (76)
	T	133 (64)	−182 (46)	−2 (13)	216 (45)
	S	−17 (28)	−2 (13)	2 (9)	33 (17)
1950	D	−720 (205)	151 (67)	−17 (32)	−242 (100)
	T	151 (67)	−206 (44)	7 (14)	269 (55)
	S	−17 (32)	7 (14)	2 (10)	44 (22)
1951	D	−693 (197)	83 (65)	−2 (35)	−229 (104)
	T	83 (65)	−129 (45)	1 (15)	303 (66)
	S	−2 (35)	1 (15)	2 (13)	55 (25)
1952	D	−617 (210)	71 (57)	24 (36)	−122 (85)
	T	72 (57)	−119 (39)	6 (13)	195 (55)
	S	24 (36)	6 (14)	2 (12)	46 (21)
1953	D	−634 (189)	70 (56)	26 (41)	−191 (79)
	T	70 (56)	−107 (39)	16 (17)	201 (52)
	S	26 (41)	16 (17)	−9 (18)	37 (25)
1954	D	−641 (175)	51 (60)	47 (39)	−171 (81)
	T	51 (60)	−101 (46)	37 (19)	171 (57)
	S	47 (39)	37 (19)	1 (17)	28 (25)

TABLE 17. MATRIX OF OWN PRICE AND CROSS SUBSTITUTION TERMS—(*cont.*)

Restricted Efficient Estimates

1949–59

Year	Dependent Variable	Independent Variables			
		P_d	P_t	P_s	P_m
1955	D	−698 (171)	48 (61)	45 (42)	−218 (85)
	T	48 (61)	−105 (47)	18 (19)	163 (60)
	S	45 (42)	18 (19)	−44 (13)	58 (30)
1956	D	−571 (164)	78 (65)	66 (52)	−165 (79)
	T	78 (65)	−144 (53)	31 (28)	140 (58)
	S	66 (52)	31 (28)	−11 (33)	71 (34)
1957	D	−589 (152)	−50 (59)	28 (48)	−150 (74)
	T	−50 (59)	−167 (49)	8 (25)	44 (64)
	S	28 (48)	8 (25)	1 (29)	73 (32)
1958	D	−573 (153)	−36 (62)	76 (46)	−165 (76)
	T	−36 (62)	−211 (55)	22 (26)	49 (71)
	S	76 (46)	22 (26)	−42 (28)	70 (36)
1959	D	−567 (141)	−59 (63)	37 (58)	−111 (63)
	T	−59 (63)	−170 (69)	−5 (35)	60 (77)
	S	37 (58)	−5 (35)	−32 (46)	72 (39)

TABLE 18. MATRIX OF OWN PRICE, CROSS, AND INCOME ELASTICITIES

Restricted Efficient Estimates

1949–59

Year	Dependent Variable	Elasticity Estimates at the Mean				
		η_{xd}	η_{xt}	η_{xs}	η_{xm}	η_{xy}
1949	D	−.34	.28	−.10	−.19	1.09
	T	.16	−.90	−.02	.67	1.12
	S	−.06	−.02	.07	.30	.69
1950	D	−.35	.30	−.09	−.31	1.05
	T	.19	−1.07	−.09	.89	1.37
	S	−.06	−.09	−.07	.38	.54
1951	D	−.32	.17	−.01	−.29	1.05
	T	.10	−.69	.02	1.01	1.18
	S	−.01	.02	.07	.43	.50
1952	D	−.28	.16	.12	−.17	1.04
	T	.08	−.67	.08	.68	1.04
	S	.06	.07	.04	.34	.50
1953	D	−.32	.17	.14	−.28	.92
	T	.08	−.63	.21	.71	1.13
	S	.06	.18	−.21	.25	.46
1954	D	−.35	.13	.26	−.26	.91
	T	.06	−.61	.47	.59	.86
	S	.10	.38	.01	.16	.32
1955	D	−.39	.13	.24	−.33	.95
	T	.06	−.65	.23	.58	.84
	S	.06	.18	−.85	.27	.45
1956	D	−.35	.23	.36	−.26	.88
	T	.11	−.96	.39	.51	.82
	S	.12	.28	−.17	.34	.49
1957	D	−.42	−.20	.17	−.27	.95
	T	−.07	−1.31	.09	.16	.71
	S	.05	.08	.01	.35	.47
1958	D	−.43	−.14	.46	−.29	.84
	T	−.05	−1.61	.25	.17	.63
	S	.14	.22	−.62	.31	.53
1959	D	−.45	−.25	.23	−.21	.96
	T	−.08	−1.32	−.05	.20	.51
	S	.06	−.05	−.44	.30	.62

TABLE 19. DEMAND DEPOSITS—TIME DEPOSITS—SAVINGS AND LOAN ASSOCIATION SHARES DEMAND FUNCTIONS

Pooled Restricted Efficient Estimates

Eq.	Y	r_d	r_t	r_s	r_m	D_m	I	A	Cal	DC	Ill	NY	W	S	C	NE
								1949–53								
D	.420	674	−98	2	97	−261	431		192	366	310	870	169	68	171	151
	(.030)	(78)	(21)	(13)	(30)	(57)	(96)		(93)	(91)	(78)	(71)	(71)	(65)	(68)	(74)
T	.163	−98	100	−2	−181	397			93	−135	5	−107	−143	−172	−129	−99
	(.019)	(21)	(14)	(5)	(19)	(36)			(46)	(47)	(43)	(40)	(33)	(28)	(31)	(33)
S	.047	2	−2	0	−24	66		.490	66	−67	139	−61	−52	−42	−15	−26
	(.008)	(13)	(5)	(5)	(8)	(14)		(.023)	(14)	(22)	(24)	(19)	(18)	(16)	(15)	(16)
								1954–58								
D	.355	600	20	−33	103	−301	448		255	519	332	823	202	93	184	110
	(.027)	(63)	(17)	(18)	(28)	(66)	(101)		(98)	(91)	(82)	(76)	(76)	(71)	(73)	(76)
T	.090	20	120	9	−114	342			136	−57	72	−69	−112	−196	−100	−102
	(.022)	(17)	(10)	(6)	(23)	(56)			(56)	(57)	(54)	(52)	(38)	(30)	(35)	(39)
S	.074	−33	9	7	−44	158		.448	−185	169	−124	−122	−118	−70	−105	−124
	(.011)	(18)	(6)	(9)	(11)	(28)		(.019)	(40)	(39)	(35)	(33)	(30)	(29)	(29)	(30)

64

APPENDIX B

Basic Data, 1949—1959

Notation	*Definition*
D	Per capita commercial bank demand deposits held by individuals, partnerships, and corporations
T	Per capita commercial bank time deposits
S	Per capita savings and loan association shares
M	Per capita mutual savings bank deposits
Y	"Permanent" per capita personal income
r_d	Actual interest rate on commercial bank demand deposits (negative)
r_t	Actual interest rate on commercial bank time deposits
r_s	Actual interest rate on savings and loan association shares
r_m	Actual interest rate on mutual savings bank deposits
A	Per capita advertising expenditures by savings and loan associations
N_c	Number of commercial bank offices per 100,000 inhabitants
N_s	Number of savings and loan association offices per 100,000 inhabitants
N_m	Number of mutual savings bank offices per 100,000 inhabitants

TABLE 20. BASIC DATA, 1949

State	D	T	S	M	Y	r_d	r_t	r_s	r_m	A	N_c	N_s	N_m
Alabama	243	86	18		697	−.213	.977	2.817		.025	8.36	.94	
Arizona	320	124	31		891	−.355	.869	1.905		.141	12.66	2.11	
Arkansas	278	49	24		616	−.207	.858	3.104		.014	7.60	.76	
California	533	489	90		1347	−.343	1.114	2.905		.163	10.39	1.66	
Colorado	590	179	81		1169	−.291	.866	2.448		.148	12.05	4.10	
Connecticut	456	200	82	651	1426	−.314	.998	2.358	1.90	.067	7.48	2.36	3.69
Delaware	1017	193	19	274	1470	−.071	.824	4.735	2.35	.013	16.61	12.54	.94
District of Columbia	854	240	338		1603	−.261	.676	2.803		.321	6.98	3.38	
Florida	408	126	103		1024	−.354	.909	2.314		.143	7.58	2.14	
Georgia	299	97	56		798	−.221	1.073	2.896		.057	13.38	2.19	
Idaho	404	163	47		931	−.274	1.407	2.380		.069	15.36	1.76	
Illinois	843	356	116		1465	−.143	.852	2.504		.191	10.63	6.99	
Indiana	418	215	101	11	1102	−.185	.952	2.376	1.53	.111	14.46	5.77	.10
Iowa	500	198	51		1087	−.248	.966	2.643		.049	31.09	3.30	
Kansas	546	84	64		1034	−.189	1.001	2.608		.084	31.38	5.30	
Kentucky	353	76	58		741	−.118	.819	2.752		.060	14.41	4.08	
Louisiana	354	104	66		819	−.170	1.016	3.084		.075	8.77	2.85	
Maine	219	213	31	257	962	−.356	1.104	2.936	1.89	.031	14.61	3.82	3.71
Maryland	413	189	96	181	1264	−.198	.869	2.986	1.85	.099	12.65	16.48	1.14
Massachusetts	555	157	140	687	1245	−.211	.918	2.627	1.93	.109	7.49	4.25	4.93
Michigan	373	335	44		1211	−.233	.846	2.172		.061	10.29	1.07	
Minnesota	459	288	77	53	1055	−.221	1.024	2.344	1.68	.118	22.81	2.36	.03
Mississippi	219	61	16		570	−.191	.880	3.094		.013	12.41	1.54	
Missouri	619	173	58		1090	−.117	.823	2.645		.058	15.06	3.93	
Montana	695	185	46		1267	−.231	.774	2.302		.030	21.02	3.60	

TABLE 20. BASIC DATA, 1949—(cont.)

State	D	T	S	M	V	r_d	r_t	r_s	r_m	A	N_c	N_s	N_m
Nebraska	694	109	38		1123	−.183	.832	2.521		.034	1.98	4.52	
Nevada	435	297	24		1204	−.178	1.281	2.978		.000	14.14	1.05	
New Hampshire	211	203	59	507	1004	−.458	1.221	3.121	2.26	.050	14.34	4.78	6.43
New Jersey	415	399	91	110	1320	−.322	.813	2.366	1.36	.074	9.67	9.93	.60
New Mexico	544	69	40		913	−.198	.849	3.043		.040	10.50	3.17	
New York	1370	271	67	768	1492	−.112	.687	2.099	1.84	.075	9.68	1.64	1.53
North Carolina	250	87	55		758	−.202	1.007	2.676		.047	10.67	4.43	
North Dakota	537	186	58		986	−.249	.991	2.019		.054	27.30	2.54	
Ohio	461	307	190	29	1206	−.202	.848	2.223	1.23	.170	10.79	7.52	.04
Oklahoma	489	52	70		865	−.211	.900	2.834		.062	16.88	2.67	
Oregon	403	206	55	9	1028	−.321	.854	2.050	1.97	.074	9.18	1.50	.06
Pennsylvania	543	274	60	100	1148	−.145	.886	2.760	1.52	.062	10.87	8.45	.23
Rhode Island	496	406	112	356	1338	−.175	1.172	2.165	1.50	.131	9.69	1.21	2.02
South Carolina	227	43	46		706	−.241	.937	2.740		.044	9.53	3.57	
South Dakota	519	130	15		956	−.244	1.089	2.489		.011	32.63	1.80	
Tennessee	309	133	36		759	−.116	1.130	2.577		.043	11.55	1.19	
Texas	573	69	36		995	−.149	.839	2.755		.038	11.77	1.89	
Utah	390	259	71		963	−.234	1.242	2.223		.159	11.17	2.72	
Vermont	212	403	36	230	938	−.495	1.582	2.733	1.72	.027	21.74	2.72	4.35
Virginia	294	179	36		960	−.225	1.051	2.598		.051	13.36	2.38	
Washington	418	201	90	74	1146	−.358	.937	2.068	1.90	.111	9.36	2.31	.23
West Virginia	245	130	22		874	−.160	1.105	2.918		.021	9.17	1.89	
Wisconsin	407	367	75	4	1116	−.231	.850	2.827	1.23	.051	20.64	4.51	.12
Wyoming	552	159	53		1197	−.246	.804	2.684		.031	18.97	3.79	

TABLE 21. BASIC DATA, 1950

State	D	T	S	M	Y	r_d	r_t	r_s	r_m	A	N_c	N_s	N_m
Alabama	252	81	20		696	−.225	.994	2.792		.034	8.07	.90	
Arizona	400	130	36		1004	−.367	.862	2.077		.144	8.53	.79	
Arkansas	305	50	29		657	−.217	.873	3.066		.017	12.89	2.22	
California	603	498	108		1464	−.364	1.162	2.935		.214	10.90	1.72	
Colorado	595	165	85		1153	−.300	.907	2.435		.169	11.73	3.86	
Connecticut	541	200	90	655	1515	−.282	1.050	2.332	1.99	.090	7.89	2.35	3.77
Delaware	1200	222	20	272	1613	−.065	.959	4.524	2.35	.015	17.96	12.69	.93
District of Columbia	1013	255	382		1773	−.267	.662	2.877		.380	7.85	3.56	
Florida	433	125	113		1007	−.342	.957	2.327		.142	7.21	2.02	
Georgia	308	89	60		791	−.246	1.086	2.873		.065	12.54	2.11	
Idaho	444	172	55		1028	−.312	1.475	2.489		.077	16.39	1.84	
Illinois	860	342	126	11	1468	−.146	.847	2.448	1.60	.231	10.05	6.52	.10
Indiana	459	220	112		1197	−.186	.969	2.381		.130	14.83	5.85	
Iowa	528	196	59		1158	−.259	.978	2.663		.060	31.02	3.30	
Kansas	571	86	73		1100	−.202	1.030	2.574		.107	31.61	5.32	
Kentucky	363	74	61		880	−.128	.805	2.758		.083	14.24	3.98	
Louisiana	371	101	74		857	−.181	1.048	3.081		.089	8.87	2.79	
Maine	229	205	34	256	984	−.372	1.124	3.004	1.95	.034	14.44	3.77	3.66
Maryland	413	172	107	169	1249	−.222	.934	2.989	1.88	.106	11.84	13.99	1.05
Massachusetts	596	151	145	695	1313	−.217	.941	2.620	2.08	.130	7.53	4.22	4.95
Michigan	448	338	51		1310	−.220	.854	2.190		.072	10.41	1.08	
Minnesota	489	278	88	55	1116	−.235	1.039	2.352	1.89	.131	22.57	2.34	.03
Mississippi	227	60	19		580	−.209	.877	3.036		.012	12.15	1.58	
Missouri	671	173	64		1142	−.120	.892	2.626		.066	14.85	3.86	
Montana	643	162	45		1230	−.259	.775	2.375		.038	18.30	3.16	

TABLE 21. BASIC DATA, 1950—(cont.)

State	D	T	S	M	Y	r_d	r_t	r_s	r_m	A	N_c	N_s	N_m
Nebraska	712	103	39		1147	−.197	.837	2.534		.047	30.66	4.16	
Nevada	572	362	31		1521	−.214	1.273	2.868		.055	16.55	1.23	
New Hampshire	242	203	71	513	1061	−.468	1.404	3.103	2.31	.092	14.21	4.80	6.46
New Jersey	475	400	109	122	1419	−.323	.849	2.356	1.56	.042	9.89	9.93	.65
New Mexico	343	63	42		879	−.204	.909	2.992		.084	9.54	2.75	
New York	1405	261	71	775	1515	−.119	.724	2.082	1.89	.053	9.42	1.57	1.50
North Carolina	264	84	60		784	−.221	1.047	2.596		.065	10.73	4.26	
North Dakota	526	177	62	30	1032	−.273	1.003	2.026	1.39	.194	27.30	2.54	.04
Ohio	524	306	206		1287	−.201	.846	2.243		.075	10.96	7.54	
Oklahoma	520	53	78	11	910	−.218	.904	2.796	1.92	.120	16.97	2.64	.06
Oregon	544	243	70		1274	−.323	1.083	2.016		.074	11.06	1.68	
Pennsylvania	601	280	69	101	1231	−.143	.894	2.752	1.51	.130	10.91	8.42	.24
Rhode Island	498	367	113	332	1294	−.189	1.258	2.209	1.83	.045	9.57	0.99	1.74
South Carolina	223	40	52		700	−.265	.944	2.800		.014	9.16	3.39	
South Dakota	528	130	17		997	−.286	1.092	2.488		.016	32.88	1.81	
Tennessee	327	131	41		790	−.120	1.165	2.571		.058	11.72	1.17	
Texas	634	71	42		1052	−.147	.836	2.740		.049	11.74	1.86	
Utah	421	255	81		1020	−.247	1.315	2.367		.174	11.29	2.71	
Vermont	226	390	37	224	948	−.490	1.693	2.706	1.90	.029	20.83	2.60	4.17
Virginia	304	172	38		951	−.239	1.146	2.626		.055	12.66	2.08	
Washington	501	216	109	83	1324	−.361	.973	2.229	1.87	.151	10.84	2.48	.25
West Virginia	252	124	24		887	−.167	1.151	2.798		.025	8.83	1.82	
Wisconsin	431	349	84	4	1161	−.241	.858	2.794	1.45	.063	20.09	4.38	.11
Wyoming	589	153	59		1275	−.251	.852	2.676		.044	17.97	3.39	

TABLE 22. BASIC DATA, 1951

State	D	T	S	M	Y	r_d	r_t	r_s	r_m	A	N_c	N_s	N_m
Alabama	268	84	24		750	−.221	1.001	2.783		.044	8.08	.89	
Arizona	426	134	41		1109	−.349	.857	1.988		.149	9.86	.75	
Arkansas	309	52	33		689	−.218	.904	3.058		.021	12.59	2.12	
California	669	530	129		1608	−.367	1.493	3.093		.264	11.09	1.75	
Colorado	598	175	97		1219	−.301	1.287	2.613		.239	11.33	3.73	
Connecticut	592	210	104	684	1669	−.265	1.175	2.383	2.12	.097	8.40	2.36	4.03
Delaware	1181	232	19	279	1795	−.070	.889	3.944	2.35	.016	18.63	12.73	.93
District of Columbia	1185	274	465		2017	−.266	.677	3.006		.421	8.73	3.70	
Florida	469	133	139		1068	−.335	1.002	2.428		.158	7.36	2.05	
Georgia	326	87	69		847	−.243	1.111	2.853		.092	12.44	2.01	
Idaho	449	184	59		1057	−.322	1.694	2.452		.081	15.90	1.59	
Illinois	887	355	144		1555	−.147	.936	2.449		.264	9.92	6.36	
Indiana	488	227	124	11	1300	−.185	.960	2.445	1.64	.144	14.73	5.66	.10
Iowa	514	196	66		1172	−.262	1.065	2.616		.072	29.52	3.18	
Kansas	592	91	83		1148	−.206	1.075	2.637		.125	30.24	5.11	
Kentucky	389	75	66		901	−.128	.888	2.760		.106	14.08	3.89	
Louisiana	409	104	83		925	−.191	1.066	3.041		.105	9.05	2.76	
Maine	249	203	35	255	1005	−.390	1.208	2.953	2.08	.032	14.52	3.66	3.55
Maryland	455	174	128	172	1376	−.234	.923	2.974	1.88	.138	12.25	13.38	1.09
Massachusetts	618	146	154	706	1390	−.215	.952	2.662	2.20	.152	7.65	4.20	4.90
Michigan	449	346	58		1414	−.224	.857	2.172		.085	10.40	1.06	
Minnesota	491	272	120	56	1169	−.255	1.081	2.547	1.90	.227	21.81	2.34	.03
Mississippi	243	60	23		623	−.209	.881	2.905		.015	12.33	1.58	
Missouri	706	179	73		1215	−.119	.932	2.639		.080	14.61	3.82	
Montana	643	155	48		1243	−.284	.798	2.349		.037	16.82	2.91	

TABLE 22. BASIC DATA, 1951—(cont.)

State	D	T	S	M	Y	r_d	r_t	r_s	r_m	A	N_c	N_s	N_m
Nebraska	714	106	44		1167	−.197	.833	2.596		.055	29.22	3.97	
Nevada	668	403	35		1725	−.273	1.258	2.839			18.13	1.25	
New Hampshire	252	199	78	505	1085	−.461	1.470	3.053	2.35	.065	13.58	4.59	6.17
New Jersey	499	404	126	132	1527	−.321	.885	2.365	1.66	.111	9.80	9.70	.64
New Mexico	332	68	45		907	−.220	1.211	2.987		.047	9.67	2.48	
New York	1409	253	85	789	1566	−.119	.795	2.218	1.90	.106	9.37	1.52	1.51
North Carolina	286	83	70		828	−.217	1.119	2.940		.070	10.75	4.13	
North Dakota	521	165	64		991	−.287	1.024	2.176		.075	25.33	2.21	
Ohio	576	322	235	32	1438	−.199	.855	2.380	1.42	.240	11.34	7.63	.04
Oklahoma	577	67	91		1003	−.226	1.230	2.823		.095	17.34	2.71	
Oregon	553	261	76	12	1373	−.325	1.289	2.050	1.95	.135	11.08	1.67	.06
Pennsylvania	626	386	78	105	1309	−.133	.910	2.733	1.90	.090	10.88	8.26	.24
Rhode Island	535	377	123	358	1422	−.186	1.235	2.321	1.93	.161	8.54	1.02	1.78
South Carolina	246	39	61		766	−.265	.946	2.921		.048	9.16	3.34	
South Dakota	506	126	19		996	−.305	1.123	2.536		.015	30.17	1.65	
Tennessee	347	137	49		848	−.121	1.247	2.624		.072	11.82	1.16	
Texas	679	77	49		1154	−.148	.812	2.819		.064	11.75	1.93	
Utah	440	256	90		1068	−.247	1.471	2.368		.209	11.35	2.57	
Vermont	246	392	41	227	992	−.496	1.737	2.709	1.92	.028	19.90	2.52	4.03
Virginia	339	180	44		1056	−.249	1.169	2.568		.061	12.89	2.07	
Washington	525	220	128	87	1433	−.365	1.039	2.367	2.16	.168	11.32	2.40	.29
West Virginia	257	124	26		926	−.163	1.180	2.788		.026	8.64	1.86	
Wisconsin	451	346	95	4	1233	−.235	.867	2.845	1.48	.077	19.37	4.22	.11
Wyoming	654	172	68		1387	−.242	1.118	2.828		.046	17.55	3.31	

TABLE 23. BASIC DATA, 1952

State	D	T	S	M	Y	r_d	r_t	r_s	r_m	A	N_e	N_s	N_m
Alabama	288	94	31		832	−.218	1.030	2.799		.059	8.49	.92	
Arizona	429	137	46		1152	−.342	.873	1.892		.184	9.37	.79	
Arkansas	334	59	41		750	−.216	1.031	3.070		.028	12.99	2.28	
California	651	530	149		1636	−.369	1.567	3.073		.316	10.47	1.62	
Colorado	607	198	121		1307	−.322	1.612	2.974		.254	11.34	3.64	
Connecticut	592	215	117	710	1763	−.263	1.268	2.489	2.31	.116	8.53	2.29	3.96
Delaware	1034	233	26	276	1829	−.080	.909	4.082	2.40	.020	19.08	11.85	.87
District of Columbia	1076	256	501		1921	−.267	.729	2.975		.493	8.06	3.37	
Florida	470	132	167		1068	−.328	1.052	2.577		.216	6.82	2.10	
Georgia	342	96	85		940	−.241	1.187	3.041		.110	12.73	2.04	
Idaho	479	225	72		1200	−.312	1.802	2.521		.102	17.03	1.67	
Illinois	914	380	175	12	1648	−.144	1.059	2.568	1.66	.338	9.88	6.32	.10
Indiana	496	238	141		1363	−.182	1.027	2.578		.171	14.38	5.49	
Iowa	551	226	82		1306	−.270	1.245	2.740		.086	31.10	3.35	
Kansas	614	109	104		1262	−.202	1.292	2.822		.132	30.14	5.13	
Kentucky	419	85	78		992	−.125	1.002	2.946		.128	14.86	4.06	
Louisiana	409	108	93		962	−.186	1.169	3.118		.117	8.89	2.64	
Maine	284	237	43	298	1174	−.367	1.440	3.067	2.46	.035	16.44	4.00	3.77
Maryland	445	168	144	164	1398	−.233	.951	3.057	2.24	.191	11.46	11.92	1.04
Massachusetts	620	144	173	755	1489	−.214	1.007	2.799	2.44	.187	7.95	4.24	5.03
Michigan	471	365	68		1480	−.230	.868	2.212		.104	10.36	1.05	
Minnesota	531	304	141	63	1272	−.255	1.288	2.382	2.08	.281	22.44	2.46	.03
Mississippi	251	62	29		662	−.203	.881	2.959		.021	12.32	1.57	
Missouri	709	187	88		1265	−.121	1.045	2.759		.114	14.17	3.62	
Montana	733	192	63		1451	−.272	.887	2.408		.047	18.35	3.20	

TABLE 23. BASIC DATA, 1952—(cont.)

State	D	T	S	M	Y	r_d	r_t	r_s	r_m	A	N_c	N_s	N_m
Nebraska	762	113	63		1260	−.195	.855	2.815		.073	29.71	4.03	
Nevada	635	377	36		1679	−.254	1.272	2.887			16.04	2.14	
New Hampshire	271	218	100	569	1211	−.452	1.590	3.207	2.60	.083	14.23	4.81	6.47
New Jersey	494	400	145	145	1603	−.324	.925	2.409	2.13	.137	9.58	9.31	.63
New Mexico	358	87	56		1042	−.234	1.575	3.241		.049	10.00	2.70	
New York	1421	272	102	860	1659	−.120	1.050	2.435	2.33	.118	9.49	1.52	1.56
North Carolina	294	90	87		889	−.209	1.232	3.019		.083	11.30	4.14	
North Dakota	585	206	91	32	1116	−.276	1.272	2.493	1.34	.108	29.41	2.35	.04
Ohio	580	323	260		1498	−.193	.893	2.446		.272	11.11	7.30	
Oklahoma	575	80	101		1029	−.221	1.483	2.908		.112	16.50	2.57	
Oregon	537	300	86	15	1421	−.338	1.750	2.462	2.36	.131	10.98	1.60	.06
Pennsylvania	637	294	93	114	1407	−.142	.974	2.837	2.00	.107	11.10	8.28	.27
Rhode Island	518	371	139	369	1471	−.188	1.286	2.574	2.17	.175	8.21	1.00	1.74
South Carolina	263	44	81		871	−.256	.971	2.994		.068	9.86	3.47	
South Dakota	570	164	27		1111	−.293	1.284	2.513		.028	34.31	2.01	
Tennessee	358	151	59		897	−.119	1.538	2.672		.089	12.01	1.21	
Texas	668	84	58		1176	−.147	1.070	2.880		.074	11.06	1.88	
Utah	459	293	104		1155	−.248	1.738	2.435		.233	11.99	2.56	
Vermont	265	436	48	253	1127	−.486	1.803	2.697	2.00	.035	20.75	2.70	4.31
Virginia	345	189	52		1122	−.244	1.226	2.849		.069	12.64	2.00	
Washington	519	230	144	95	1481	−.381	1.305	2.553	2.41	.193	11.12	2.39	.28
West Virginia	279	140	32	5	1023	−.161	1.259	2.919	1.53	.028	9.08	1.80	.11
Wisconsin	490	371	123		1352	−.226	.907	3.080		.102	19.67	4.29	
Wyoming	655	198	74		1462	−.245	1.472	2.545		.046	17.16	3.30	

TABLE 24. BASIC DATA, 1953

State	D	T	S	M	Y	r_d	r_t	r_s	r_m	A	N_c	N_e	N_m
Alabama	288	100	37		867	−.237	1.126	2.854		.074	8.44	1.00	
Arizona	408	154	61		1206	−.375	1.300	2.466		.245	9.24	2.04	
Arkansas	344	70	51		805	−.223	1.304	3.087		.035	13.47	2.42	
California	609	520	177		1669	−.410	1.594	3.357		.335	10.06	1.99	
Colorado	584	215	147		1359	−.352	1.636	3.118		.250	11.26	4.11	
Connecticut	565	211	128	712	1781	−.292	1.347	2.553	2.36	.129	8.17	2.35	3.91
Delaware	1053	240	29	288	1911	−.089	.998	3.664	2.86	.022	19.17	11.11	.83
District of Columbia	1004	258	543		1856	−.287	.883	3.035		.637	8.02	3.67	
Florida	464	138	200		1138	−.354	1.118	2.625		.295	6.72	2.52	
Georgia	342	103	103		989	−.268	1.351	3.105		.137	12.64	2.29	
Idaho	448	248	79		1223	−.329	1.914	2.603		.087	17.00	1.65	
Illinois	909	396	209		1711	−.150	1.091	2.703		.424	9.75	6.21	
Indiana	508	255	165	12	1470	−.195	1.105	2.687	1.64	.183	14.54	5.68	.09
Iowa	590	255	100		1349	−.273	1.383	2.800		.101	31.78	3.42	
Kansas	590	125	125		1313	−.217	1.530	2.902		.155	29.84	5.19	
Kentucky	411	93	88		1020	−.139	1.117	3.071		.149	14.65	4.28	
Louisiana	424	115	108		1033	−.195	1.260	3.097		.145	9.26	2.65	
Maine	270	240	46	309	1196	−.403	1.542	3.177	2.49	.045	16.42	3.80	3.69
Maryland	434	172	173	172	1508	−.263	1.019	3.084	2.29	.209	11.52	14.36	1.07
Massachusetts	596	135	190	772	1508	−.240	1.063	2.949	2.65	.176	7.86	4.20	4.92
Michigan	482	388	81		1592	−.243	.891	2.253		.132	10.46	1.46	
Minnesota	530	320	158	67	1317	−.272	1.399	2.502	2.17	.325	22.02	2.62	.03
Mississippi	275	65	37		712	−.207	.881	3.028		.026	12.83	1.62	
Missouri	718	205	116		1361	−.130	1.230	2.926		.152	14.41	3.80	
Montana	676	189	69		1417	−.293	.975	2.534		.058	17.17	2.99	

TABLE 24. BASIC DATA, 1953—(cont.)

State	D	T	S	M	Y	r_d	r_t	r_s	r_m	A	N_c	N_s	N_m
Nebraska	784	120	86		1301	−.197	.908	2.873		.082	30.20	4.08	
Nevada	611	371	37		1679	−.262	1.283	2.874			14.35	1.91	
New Hampshire	274	228	121	628	1310	−.502	1.826	3.235	2.76	.087	14.56	4.91	6.62
New Jersey	489	406	168	159	1703	−.347	.974	2.463	2.03	.146	9.73	9.39	.62
New Mexico	335	95	66		1082	−.256	1.623	3.470		.066	9.97	2.85	
New York	1395	296	118	928	1744	−.134	1.241	2.477	2.40	.134	9.66	1.88	1.58
North Carolina	289	95	105		931	−.231	1.332	3.006		.098	11.61	4.17	
North Dakota	557	217	105		1101	−.304	1.395	2.469		.166	29.12	2.33	
Ohio	570	335	281	34	1557	−.205	1.061	2.527	1.83	.312	10.95	7.64	.04
Oklahoma	601	102	122		1138	−.241	1.538	2.973		.136	17.21	2.86	
Oregon	499	323	95	15	1455	−.382	1.778	2.550	2.37	.157	10.98	1.81	.06
Pennsylvania	634	305	110	120	1487	−.154	1.054	2.377	2.02	.129	11.21	8.09	.28
Rhode Island	472	359	150	377	1476	−.212	1.350	2.608	2.23	.179	8.03	1.53	2.01
South Carolina	249	45	97		907	−.286	1.046	3.090		.083	9.92	3.32	
South Dakota	564	184	32		1138	−.302	1.456	2.550		.037	34.26	2.02	
Tennessee	370	171	73		976	−.128	1.643	2.739		.114	12.62	1.30	
Texas	666	99	73		1228	−.160	1.170	3.082		.097	10.93	2.03	
Utah	454	306	129		1199	−.275	1.833	2.841		.309	11.91	3.14	
Vermont	251	439	56	257	1167	−.547	1.848	3.026	2.12	.042	20.42	2.39	4.24
Virginia	328	198	62		1161	−.276	1.451	2.893		.076	12.72	2.10	
Washington	500	235	174	100	1531	−.414	1.342	2.848	2.43	.207	11.08	2.72	.31
West Virginia	293	152	38		1101	−.170	1.320	2.936		.036	9.46	1.98	
Wisconsin	488	383	150	5	1412	−.238	.963	3.114	1.56	.113	19.48	4.28	.11
Wyoming	581	208	80		1408	−.268	1.341	2.780		.046	15.95	3.07	

75

TABLE 25. BASIC DATA, 1954

State	D	T	S	M	Y	r_d	r_t	r_s	r_m	A	N_c	N_s	N_m
Alabama	290	104	46		873	−.258	1.256	2.870		.080	8.56	1.14	
Arizona	390	158	73		1145	−.454	1.716	2.831		.191	8.96	1.81	
Arkansas	332	77	58		781	−.233	1.575	3.041		.041	12.91	2.45	
California	634	543	213	764	1716	−.499	1.609	3.295	2.42	.419	9.96	2.23	4.04
Colorado	642	235	194	295	1433	−.381	1.645	3.262	2.75	.347	11.32	4.57	.80
Connecticut	577	218	148		1880	−.319	1.379	2.564		.155	8.53	2.40	
Delaware	1023	246	33		1934	−.099	1.159	3.532		.029	17.77	10.61	
District of Columbia	1044	305	626		1868	−.308	1.500	3.083		.774	8.14	4.13	
Florida	465	140	247		1137	−.374	1.268	2.871		.319	6.37	2.60	
Georgia	339	110	119		996	−.302	1.553	3.112		.164	12.31	2.35	
Idaho	455	259	86		1192	−.365	1.837	2.594		.108	16.38	1.59	
Illinois	928	414	253	13	1775	−.164	1.130	2.748	1.66	.502	9.81	6.19	.09
Indiana	520	260	189		1517	−.207	1.153	2.725		.207	14.72	5.69	
Iowa	568	264	116		1365	−.283	1.483	2.876		.127	30.76	3.39	
Kansas	605	138	151		1380	−.233	1.635	2.970		.211	29.69	5.30	
Kentucky	415	98	104		1016	−.146	1.188	3.183		.161	14.30	4.26	
Louisiana	425	120	122		1032	−.207	1.342	3.096		.173	9.12	2.60	
Maine	257	230	47	307	1147	−.440	1.593	3.347	2.51	.040	15.75	3.55	3.44
Maryland	450	181	208	178	1579	−.308	1.250	3.295	2.43	.229	11.68	14.14	1.18
Massachusetts	620	137	215	827	1563	−.272	1.059	3.000	2.80	.197	8.16	4.26	4.97
Michigan	478	397	94		1634	−.284	.948	2.276		.167	10.60	1.52	
Minnesota	536	332	187	70	1354	−.297	1.473	2.814	2.32	.318	21.69	2.60	.03
Mississippi	258	73	45		698	−.219	1.143	3.165		.038	12.59	1.73	
Missouri	715	217	146		1388	−.144	1.339	3.004		.163	14.11	3.81	
Montana	693	201	84		1445	−.332	1.144	2.693		.064	17.24	2.98	

TABLE 25. BASIC DATA, 1954—(cont.)

State	D	T	S	M	Y	r_d	r_t	r_s	r_m	A	N_c	N_s	N_m
Nebraska	771	121	102		1345	−.208	.977	2.755		.114	29.98	4.13	
Nevada	624	369	41		1696	−.283	1.257	3.340		.017	13.91	1.74	
New Hampshire	279	232	137	669	1356	−.520	1.302	3.159	2.87	.109	14.47	4.82	6.49
New Jersey	512	412	208	176	1787	−.380	1.028	2.577	2.21	.170	10.05	9.47	.66
New Mexico	347	105	79		1104	−.304	1.614	3.564		.071	9.75	2.88	
New York	1415	318	135	991	1802	−.145	1.346	2.540	2.49	.131	9.73	1.93	1.60
North Carolina	301	99	124		967	−.253	1.372	2.984		.116	12.29	4.24	
North Dakota	508	204	110		1006	−.336	1.444	2.436		.203	26.78	2.27	
Ohio	575	349	321	43	1640	−.242	1.217	2.644	1.68	.353	11.17	7.77	.15
Oklahoma	597	118	136		1143	−.255	1.636	3.022		.135	16.67	2.77	
Oregon	533	355	108	17	1492	−.461	1.780	2.633	2.41	.143	11.10	1.87	.06
Pennsylvania	642	323	131	126	1523	−.171	1.128	2.953	2.13	.147	11.47	8.11	.33
Rhode Island	500	362	169	426	1556	−.238	1.360	2.554	2.43	.209	8.71	1.57	2.78
South Carolina	240	47	115		908	−.321	1.135	3.102		.099	10.06	3.38	
South Dakota	544	193	36		1108	−.320	1.589	2.691		.045	32.46	1.90	
Tennessee	365	181	87		982	−.139	1.711	2.870		.132	12.30	1.37	
Texas	708	117	92		1285	−.182	1.328	3.093		.116	10.99	2.14	
Utah	485	326	154		1246	−.295	1.873	2.887		.314	11.99	3.39	
Vermont	242	437	62	261	1152	−.613	1.882	3.029	2.31	.046	19.54	2.28	4.06
Virginia	343	214	76		1204	−.315	1.582	2.977		.092	13.04	2.43	
Washington	537	247	213	108	1602	−.481	1.348	2.865	2.44	.191	11.40	2.88	.31
West Virginia	284	151	43		1078	−.174	1.359	2.976		.042	9.28	1.93	
Wisconsin	501	388	184	5	1449	−.253	1.025	3.152	1.57	.155	19.35	4.25	.11
Wyoming	633	232	96		1490	−.291	1.595	2.820		.058	17.31	3.21	

TABLE 26. BASIC DATA, 1955

State	D	T	S	M	Y	r_d	r_t	r_s	r_m	A	N_c	N_s	N_m
Alabama	331	111	58		958	−.261	1.313	2.860		.109	9.24	1.20	
Arizona	438	183	99		1277	−.461	1.705	2.832		.310	10.24	2.78	
Arkansas	383	92	74		879	−.240	1.588	3.039		.058	14.23	2.60	
California	665	549	256	810	1779	−.496	1.637	3.451		.508	10.16	2.29	
Colorado	615	229	229	295	1412	−.408	1.716	3.246		.427	10.79	4.51	
Connecticut	622	220	166		1969	−.327	1.470	2.648	2.57	.192	8.79	2.42	4.04
Delaware	1128	248	37		1962	−.100	1.190	3.528	2.84	.030	17.09	9.80	.75
District of Columbia	1067	329	722		1931	−.318	1.504	3.177		.824	8.22	4.51	
Florida	545	161	334		1306	−.378	1.339	2.882		.449	7.01	3.01	
Georgia	374	118	141		1079	−.317	1.601	3.125		.205	12.79	2.57	
Idaho	454	270	105		1238	−.391	1.814	2.820		.131	16.69	1.62	
Illinois	939	414	296		1815	−.172	1.141	2.778		.537	9.68	6.07	
Indiana	529	260	209	12	1537	−.214	1.180	2.754	1.64	.237	14.50	5.54	.09
Iowa	545	263	132		1348	−.301	1.532	2.899		.144	30.35	3.37	
Kansas	568	142	182		1384	−.254	1.671	3.085		.300	28.89	5.27	
Kentucky	432	103	122		1030	−.153	1.251	3.152		.198	14.82	4.37	
Louisiana	455	128	143		1091	−.213	1.395	3.102		.209	9.84	2.60	
Maine	296	249	56	344	1269	−.450	1.584	3.329	2.67	.045	16.79	3.71	3.71
Maryland	467	180	241	181	1634	−.337	1.310	3.314	2.51	.225	11.81	13.95	1.26
Massachusetts	642	135	237	881	1615	−.289	1.081	3.008	2.84	.229	8.63	4.28	5.03
Michigan	517	406	109		1702	−.295	1.010	2.342		.188	10.75	1.55	
Minnesota	532	334	221	72	1385	−.324	1.498	2.872	2.43	.403	21.31	2.55	.03
Mississippi	296	81	59		773	−.228	1.330	3.105		.053	13.84	1.97	
Missouri	757	227	177		1477	−.166	1.355	3.120		.203	14.40	4.09	
Montana	686	211	97		1483	−.356	1.219	2.703		.074	17.49	3.10	

TABLE 26. BASIC DATA, 1955—(cont.)

State	D	T	S	M	Y	r_d	r_i	r_s	r_m	A	N_o	N_s	N_m
Nebraska	735	116	121		1336	−.229	1.023	2.848		.165	29.69	4.15	
Nevada	627	372	55		1863	−.311	1.253	3.524		.017	14.96	1.71	
New Hampshire	298	232	149	699	1372	−.522	2.000	3.259	2.90	.138	13.81	4.42	6.19
New Jersey	531	404	239	184	1825	−.399	1.189	2.628	2.30	.205	10.08	9.12	.67
New Mexico	359	113	95		1157	−.375	1.592	3.498		.073	10.07	2.99	
New York	1431	313	149	1011	1808	−.146	1.406	2.655	2.67	.145	9.43	1.86	1.55
North Carolina	320	101	143		1006	−.266	1.436	2.991		.138	12.57	4.23	
North Dakota	505	209	128		1082	−.356	1.511	2.505		.280	27.43	2.31	
Ohio	585	342	351	41	1647	−.257	1.254	2.779	1.72	.388	10.87	7.39	.15
Oklahoma	654	125	163		1259	−.279	1.689	3.023		.180	17.68	2.92	
Oregon	535	369	123	18	1513	−.471	1.803	2.738	2.40	.160	11.37	1.83	.06
Pennsylvania	654	315	149	132	1524	−.183	1.165	2.954	2.46	.167	11.37	7.82	.34
Rhode Island	524	358	180	443	1565	−.252	1.588	2.628	2.42	.225	9.15	1.53	2.82
South Carolina	249	47	135		929	−.344	1.215	3.080		.137	10.17	3.42	
South Dakota	524	200	46		1101	−.335	1.653	2.795		.054	32.89	2.05	
Tennessee	378	192	101		1017	−.143	1.859	2.872		.177	12.52	1.47	
Texas	722	127	111		1335	−.191	1.368	3.071		.137	11.00	2.26	
Utah	474	325	198	289	1264	−.313	1.918	3.058	2.48	.452	12.03	3.51	4.45
Vermont	276	460	71		1233	−.636	1.999	3.035		.055	19.90	2.36	
Virginia	363	228	88		1259	−.327	1.601	2.847		.110	13.59	2.57	
Washington	545	266	246	111	1649	−.529	1.770	2.907	2.68	.278	11.95	3.07	.35
West Virginia	287	149	50		1071	−.180	1.377	2.973		.052	8.93	1.88	
Wisconsin	501	376	219	5	1456	−.264	1.049	3.214	1.75	.176	18.67	4.11	.11
Wyoming	597	242	107		1500	−.317	1.677	2.876		.064	17.20	3.18	

TABLE 27. BASIC DATA, 1956

State	D	T	S	M	Y	r_d	r_t	r_s	r_m	A	N_c	N_s	N_n
Alabama	323	117	68		990	−.281	1.496	2.915		.138	9.16	1.33	
Arizona	464	183	109		1304	−.492	1.669	2.888		.339	11.03	2.85	
Arkansas	383	98	84		899	−.262	1.700	3.086		.067	14.29	2.56	
California	676	539	306	879	1878	−.533	1.757	3.539		.704	10.43	2.46	
Colorado	596	229	261		1450	−.464	1.797	3.316		.510	10.57	4.71	
Connecticut	652	227	189		2131	−.337	1.675	2.773	2.75	.213	9.42	2.43	4.33
Delaware	1064	264	40	302	2163	−.107	1.206	3.309	2.87	.041	16.59	9.51	.73
District of Columbia	1062	330	786		1951	−.322	1.598	3.250		.895	8.11	4.79	
Florida	567	166	383		1339	−.399	1.486	3.032		.553	6.94	3.09	
Georgia	367	125	160		1119	−.336	1.967	3.311		.242	12.74	2.58	
Idaho	464	268	120		1275	−.430	1.858	2.918		.162	16.51	2.36	
Illinois	944	427	350		1915	−.183	1.354	2.932		.676	9.72	6.08	
Indiana	528	270	230	12	1594	−.231	1.408	2.841	1.64	.308	14.75	5.60	.09
Iowa	562	267	154		1394	−.326	1.604	2.958		.229	30.45	3.38	
Kansas	565	149	201		1406	−.305	1.757	3.018		.395	28.11	5.29	
Kentucky	447	110	139		1080	−.166	1.405	3.180		.234	15.17	4.41	
Louisiana	474	140	160		1139	−.236	1.592	3.173		.267	10.11	2.68	
Maine	308	256	62	366	1346	−.471	1.660	3.402	2.75	.059	17.45	3.71	3.71
Maryland	455	177	262	179	1660	−.367	1.476	3.321	2.58	.261	11.53	13.31	1.26
Massachusetts	680	135	269	981	1782	−.308	1.379	3.012	2.86	.276	9.30	4.55	5.57
Michigan	489	407	121		1741	−.328	1.252	2.549		.221	10.76	1.63	
Minnesota	543	339	248	78	1425	−.370	1.642	2.967	2.75	.540	20.91	2.62	.03
Mississippi	292	87	72		806	−.267	1.521	3.132		.068	14.02	2.30	
Missouri	743	232	198		1515	−.186	1.427	3.049		.279	14.16	4.04	
Montana	692	243	111		1546	−.392	1.682	2.883		.099	17.47	3.09	

TABLE 27. BASIC DATA, 1956—(cont.)

State	D	T	S	M	Y	r_d	r_t	r_s	r_m	A	N_c	N_s	N_m
Nebraska	718	111	140		1338	−.250	1.133	2.952		.257	29.12	4.05	
Nevada	597	389	67		1867	−.375	1.732	3.338		.059	13.73	1.96	
New Hampshire	314	226	163	759	1439	−.545	2.164	3.123	3.00	.201	13.40	4.59	6.17
New Jersey	555	431	271	201	1955	−.448	1.572	2.707	2.51	.252	10.61	9.17	.71
New Mexico	383	122	108		1199	−.396	1.596	3.488		.078	10.47	3.01	
New York	1416	339	168	1078	1915	−.168	1.754	2.774	2.81	.169	9.71	1.91	1.58
North Carolina	315	105	156		1041	−.290	1.756	3.049		.166	12.72	4.14	
North Dakota	535	211	150		1103	−.375	1.636	2.668		.379	26.95	2.25	
Ohio	592	354	394	35	1731	−.273	1.343	2.929	1.85	.449	11.40	7.51	.15
Oklahoma	646	134	174		1281	−.314	1.853	3.044		.208	17.27	2.83	
Oregon	509	362	139	17	1558	−.548	1.805	2.875	2.45	.165	11.52	1.83	.06
Pennsylvania	680	338	176	146	1640	−.200	1.444	2.960	2.58	.214	12.00	8.05	.37
Rhode Island	513	370	207	470	1648	−.295	1.767	2.942	2.57	.231	9.77	1.67	2.98
South Carolina	242	50	150		933	−.377	1.428	3.112		.151	10.17	3.39	
South Dakota	500	199	54		1088	−.368	1.764	2.899		.065	31.82	1.98	
Tennessee	387	200	113		1063	−.157	1.939	2.889		.206	12.70	1.54	
Texas	708	132	124		1358	−.208	1.544	3.063		.176	10.71	2.36	
Utah	477	337	210		1307	−.334	2.143	2.949		.526	12.36	3.76	
Vermont	314	482	80	324	1328	−.638	2.104	3.038	2.58	.073	20.43	2.42	4.57
Virginia	370	236	98		1309	−.356	1.751	2.939		.136	13.78	2.54	
Washington	525	268	263	113	1656	−.587	1.779	3.011	2.80	.273	11.87	3.13	.41
West Virginia	311	156	58		1151	−.183	1.521	2.943		.061	9.13	1.91	
Wisconsin	510	381	249	5	1507	−.289	1.288	3.250	1.84	.219	18.28	4.03	.10
Wyoming	590	244	120		1503	−.349	1.873	3.023		.070	16.46	3.05	

TABLE 28. BASIC DATA, 1957

State	D	T	S	M	Y	r_d	r_t	r_s	r_m	A	N_o	N_s	N_m
Alabama	314	142	81		1051	−.325	2.397	3.323		.169	9.39	1.41	
Arizona	451	200	114		1330	−.586	2.151	3.020		.268	11.31	3.17	
Arkansas	380	117	101		956	−.292	2.148	3.417		.079	14.88	2.64	
California	642	586	350	922	1963	−.630	2.641	3.930	2.85	.829	10.59	2.79	4.65
Colorado	580	242	279		1530	−.538	2.160	3.362		.554	10.56	4.63	
Connecticut	627	238	204		2258	−.402	2.009	2.892		.245	9.91	2.50	
Delaware	958	258	43	293	2131	−.129	1.607	3.548	3.10	.049	15.33	8.67	.89
District of Columbia	1120	391	898		2085	−.346	2.231	3.368		1.222	8.74	5.03	
Florida	531	214	418		1383	−.447	2.420	3.338		.662	6.62	3.00	
Georgia	359	146	175		1152	−.395	2.555	3.506		.286	12.55	2.63	
Idaho	449	304	133		1315	−.652	2.713	3.344		.203	16.28	2.61	
Illinois	899	442	392		1980	−.203	1.628	3.155		.747	9.62	6.02	
Indiana	507	275	248	12	1629	−.262	1.666	2.983	1.72	.335	14.89	5.51	.09
Iowa	557	285	165		1422	−.347	1.904	3.148		.228	29.26	3.21	
Kansas	542	172	222		1446	−.364	2.052	3.266		.402	27.73	5.13	
Kentucky	443	124	157		1114	−.190	1.808	3.375		.264	15.34	4.52	
Louisiana	462	166	179		1217	−.264	2.396	3.559		.260	10.38	2.79	
Maine	289	255	63	369	1355	−.524	2.062	3.362	2.83	.065	17.59	3.56	3.66
Maryland	430	291	277	183	1725	−.433	2.083	3.378	2.89	.315	11.54	13.48	1.32
Massachusetts	667	138	286	1011	1861	−.348	1.779	3.075	2.97	.310	9.49	4.49	5.63
Michigan	460	410	140		1752	−.371	1.604	2.903		.228	10.58	1.70	
Minnesota	521	372	269	81	1472	−.410	2.017	3.164	2.92	.500	20.42	2.67	.03
Mississippi	269	104	77		798	−.315	2.117	3.260		.071	14.05	2.35	
Missouri	739	253	225		1583	−.205	1.723	3.319		.366	14.13	4.43	
Montana	646	283	120		1544	−.439	2.125	2.946		.108	16.99	2.95	

TABLE 28. BASIC DATA, 1957—(cont.)

State	D	T	S	M	Y	r_d	r_t	r_s	r_m	A	N_c	N_s	N_m
Nebraska	679	110	154		1397	−.275	1.300	3.055		.221	28.31	3.87	
Nevada	549	429	87		1872	−.426	2.226	3.782		.120	13.87	1.82	
New Hampshire	302	228	175	778	1492	−.587	2.563	3.241	3.02	.223	13.30	4.49	6.04
New Jersey	525	448	293	207	1992	−.491	1.947	2.938	2.73	.277	10.54	8.80	.68
New Mexico	390	133	121		1285	−.427	1.990	3.480		.114	10.77	2.96	
New York	1443	400	189	1165	2074	−.189	2.231	2.957	2.99	.193	10.21	2.03	1.64
North Carolina	298	117	173		1070	−.331	2.077	3.309		.180	13.07	4.20	
North Dakota	558	280	176		1190	−.376	2.081	2.894		.446	27.78	2.31	
Ohio	579	368	434	34	1814	−.311	1.686	3.111	2.09	.535	11.33	7.59	.16
Oklahoma	644	156	190		1318	−.357	2.396	3.398		.200	17.05	2.82	
Oregon	470	368	145	21	1567	−.662	2.283	3.010	2.94	.224	11.75	2.06	.06
Pennsylvania	660	362	194	155	1710	−.229	1.829	3.014	2.77	.254	12.23	3.09	.43
Rhode Island	465	374	216	479	1625	−.413	2.482	3.098	2.91	.241	9.94	1.83	3.31
South Carolina	238	59	166		963	−.409	2.022	3.297		.166	10.57	3.41	
South Dakota	504	244	60		1180	−.403	2.062	2.960		.090	31.65	2.11	
Tennessee	379	227	126		1124	−.187	2.406	3.204		.218	13.21	1.63	
Texas	675	159	144		1416	−.250	2.121	3.487		.195	10.59	2.61	
Utah	424	340	220	329	1328	−.494	2.547	3.374	2.86	.459	13.23	4.14	4.46
Vermont	296	507	84		1349	−.692	2.570	3.209		.092	19.95	2.36	
Virginia	359	252	106	119	1328	−.382	2.155	3.141	2.91	.137	13.72	2.43	.40
Washington	494	287	285		1711	−.681	2.313	3.252		.327	12.02	3.19	
West Virginia	315	166	66		1225	−.205	1.794	2.941		.091	9.18	1.91	
Wisconsin	499	403	276	5	1544	−.323	1.713	3.542	2.15	.220	17.83	3.93	.10
Wyoming	624	287	137		1642	−.394	2.360	3.032		.091	16.98	3.14	

83

TABLE 29. BASIC DATA, 1958

State	D	T	S	M	Y	r_d	r_t	r_s	r_m	A	N_c	N_s	N_m
Alabama	330	162	93		1088	−.364	2.495	3.350		.215	9.26	1.57	
Arizona	503	238	132		1446	−.612	2.209	2.977		.389	12.32	3.74	
Arkansas	415	136	119		1001	−.317	2.288	3.421		.095	15.33	2.71	
California	678	636	417		2034	−.667	2.641	3.982		.835	10.80	2.92	
Colorado	616	284	320		1602	−.573	2.511	3.662		.588	10.72	4.64	
Connecticut	617	246	217	960	2283	−.439	2.196	2.923	2.95	.277	10.17	2.55	4.81
Delaware	922	268	49	306	2180	−.139	1.686	3.587	3.35	.062	15.24	8.37	.86
District of Columbia	1196	437	1012		2144	−.360	2.100	3.457		1.242	8.77	5.05	
Florida	533	240	447		1409	−.498	2.453	3.353		.749	6.33	3.27	
Georgia	380	167	200		1200	−.452	2.619	3.588		.268	12.59	2.69	
Idaho	472	331	159		1347	−.678	2.758	3.650		.227	16.17	3.41	
Illinois	919	464	444		2001	−.214	1.737	3.402		.804	9.44	5.84	
Indiana	516	289	275	12	1655	−.286	1.731	3.099	1.76	.371	15.21	5.60	.09
Iowa	614	315	187		1490	−.361	2.192	3.246		.240	29.14	3.19	
Kansas	593	197	255		1566	−.394	2.136	3.316		.410	28.44	5.15	
Kentucky	452	137	179		1145	−.210	1.975	3.628		.275	15.29	4.46	
Louisiana	476	187	208		1271	−.304	2.479	3.799		.208	10.87	2.86	
Maine	298	280	70	390	1402	−.536	2.361	3.494	2.88	.058	18.17	3.53	3.63
Maryland	443	204	316	189	1792	−.465	2.211	3.751	2.90	.327	11.66	13.43	1.33
Massachusetts	700	145	309	1078	1951	−.363	1.901	3.129	3.10	.307	10.05	4.55	5.79
Michigan	450	440	160		1774	−.401	1.783	2.951		.233	11.08	1.77	
Minnesota	553	404	306	88	1532	−.437	2.270	3.374	3.20	.547	20.20	2.66	.03
Mississippi	295	125	88		841	−.354	2.415	3.510		.072	14.41	2.54	
Missouri	780	279	265		1649	−.217	1.851	3.434		.427	14.23	4.46	
Montana	655	313	132		1564	−.475	2.208	2.962		.119	16.43	2.71	

TABLE 29. BASIC DATA, 1958—(cont.)

State	D	T	S	M	Y	r_d	r_t	r_s	r_m	A	N_c	N_s	N_m
Nebraska	782	122	177		1490	−.282	1.473	3.080		.255	28.43	3.93	
Nevada	596	503	115		2030	−.458	2.597	3.808		.114	14.39	1.85	
New Hampshire	309	243	190	812	1530	−.639	2.753	3.296	3.23	.218	13.18	4.39	5.91
New Jersey	532	475	327	219	2033	−.512	2.061	3.057	2.82	.275	10.71	8.64	.70
New Mexico	434	153	140		1386	−.460	2.150	4.220		.113	11.15	2.67	
New York	1453	452	206	1230	2120	−.192	2.360	3.073	3.13	.199	10.18	2.01	1.63
North Carolina	322	130	197		1116	−.367	2.191	3.383		.145	13.34	4.27	
North Dakota	591	326	196		1270	−.377	2.461	2.953		.471	27.74	2.59	
Ohio	576	382	469	34	1831	−.342	1.884	3.181	2.33	.591	12.23	7.62	.18
Oklahoma	692	183	213		1385	−.374	2.446	3.372		.226	17.36	2.86	
Oregon	510	408	165	23	1624	−.695	2.344	3.282	2.95	.208	12.19	1.95	.06
Pennsylvania	665	396	217	169	1756	−.242	2.042	3.171	2.92	.284	12.60	8.12	.46
Rhode Island	459	404	231	499	1635	−.533	2.649	3.244	2.93	.220	10.47	1.91	3.38
South Carolina	254	66	186		987	−.458	2.113	3.412		.192	11.18	3.45	
South Dakota	590	293	75		1271	−.412	2.371	3.168		.104	32.06	2.13	
Tennessee	412	262	144		1177	−.234	2.593	3.335		.233	13.66	1.83	
Texas	716	201	165		1457	−.278	2.241	3.413		.211	10.44	2.77	
Utah	441	386	240	283	1387	−.587	2.602	3.372	3.05	.543	15.27	4.42	1.87
Vermont	303	632	91		1424	−.756	2.694	3.218		.104	23.20	2.40	
Virginia	364	273	116		1348	−.413	2.314	3.265		.141	13.62	2.15	
Washington	521	309	318	127	1754	−.716	2.302	3.306	2.92	.375	12.19	3.35	.39
West Virginia	333	187	75		1261	−.222	1.931	3.106		.082	9.23	1.92	
Wisconsin	516	442	304	6	1577	−.338	2.084	3.615	2.50	.224	17.54	3.85	.10
Wyoming	653	329	156		1697	−.414	2.463	3.220		.118	16.41	3.10	

TABLE 30. BASIC DATA, 1959

State	D	T	S	M	Y	r_d	r_t	r_s	r_m	A	N_c	N_s	N_m
Alabama	340	174	113		1163	−.407	2.602	3.619		.252	9.78	1.71	
Arizona	506	263	155		1470	−.662	2.565	3.558		.384	12.15	2.13	
Arkansas	437	158	136		1081	−.335	2.547	3.469		.147	15.79	2.80	
California	714	643	494	974	2164	−.664	2.648	4.047		1.062	11.17	3.11	
Colorado	631	308	368		1757	−.608	2.524	3.654		.771	11.33	5.17	
Connecticut	597	239	227		2303	−.478	2.332	3.193	3.21	.300	10.49	2.57	4.90
Delaware	938	288	56	329	2332	−.161	1.747	3.543	3.37	.065	15.84	8.46	1.08
District of Columbia	1168	404	1129		2167	−.418	2.342	3.727		1.298	8.95	5.18	
Florida	522	235	510		1457	−.523	2.489	3.575		.807	6.20	3.45	
Georgia	387	176	220		1266	−.501	2.668	3.591		.350	12.89	2.86	
Idaho	467	342	188		1428	−.677	2.750	3.782		.266	16.79	3.86	
Illinois	874	475	489		2035	−.231	2.054	3.497		.910	9.24	5.67	
Indiana	517	292	302	12	1706	−.296	1.800	3.286	1.76	.415	15.45	5.56	.09
Iowa	586	330	211		1564	−.382	2.341	3.333		.338	29.74	3.28	
Kansas	565	211	289		1612	−.413	2.332	3.578		.449	28.35	5.69	
Kentucky	448	145	200		1183	−.220	2.092	3.622		.311	15.54	4.50	
Louisiana	463	197	232		1315	−.339	2.507	3.822		.245	10.88	3.02	
Maine	303	295	79	416	1477	−.573	2.462	3.673	3.16	.073	18.51	3.35	3.97
Maryland	437	210	341	186	1858	−.486	2.274	3.832	3.00	.355	11.89	13.51	1.30
Massachusetts	688	143	328	1105	2017	−.396	1.988	3.264	3.23	.314	10.45	4.46	5.96
Michigan	455	455	180		1815	−.439	2.118	3.117		.266	11.35	1.86	
Minnesota	532	415	342	91	1591	−.470	2.432	3.447	3.24	.634	20.10	2.70	.03
Mississippi	315	140	101		905	−.380	2.600	3.694		.092	14.72	2.94	
Missouri	778	296	311		1755	−.236	2.036	3.665		.504	14.70	4.63	
Montana	624	339	153		1611	−.506	2.316	3.386		.147	16.67	2.59	

TABLE 30. BASIC DATA, 1959—(cont).

State	D	T	S	M	Y	r_d	r_t	r_s	r_m	A	N_c	N_s	N_m
Nebraska	718	139	197		1557	−.290	1.989	3.248		.346	28.72	3.87	
Nevada	651	529	136		2081	−.472	2.573	3.901		.102	15.09	1.75	5.84
New Hampshire	338	236	210	846	1608	−.670	3.210	3.414	3.31	.237	13.02	4.34	.68
New Jersey	538	486	359	218	2082	−.536	2.191	3.206	2.93	.314	10.85	8.59	
New Mexico	431	162	153		1458	−.512	2.342	3.714		.135	11.28	2.79	1.61
New York	1417	454	223	1244	2197	−.203	2.521	3.223	3.22	.242	10.29	2.01	
North Carolina	335	135	228		1192	−.397	2.207	3.514		.266	14.06	4.56	
North Dakota	574	360	230		1306	−.396	2.598	3.157		.505	28.28	2.63	.05
Ohio	557	413	501	3	1841	−.369	2.212	3.431	2.29	.619	12.07	7.79	
Oklahoma	682	201	250		1467	−.401	2.566	3.657		.239	17.63	2.87	.06
Oregon	524	435	185	24	1735	−.740	2.518	3.324	3.19	.291	12.96	2.52	.47
Pennsylvania	648	404	236	175	1789	−.269	2.141	3.304	3.02	.312	12.76	8.04	3.62
Rhode Island	475	423	245	533	1709	−.542	2.671	3.341	3.19	.252	11.20	1.92	
South Carolina	264	69	204		1041	−.488	2.206	3.427		.244	11.43	3.57	
South Dakota	572	324	91		1296	−.408	2.524	3.327		.116	32.80	2.17	
Tennessee	427	274	161		1231	−.253	2.688	3.449		.269	13.90	1.90	
Texas	703	211	196		1520	−.303	2.435	3.671		.269	10.55	2.94	
Utah	453	392	273		1458	−.620	2.619	3.610		.736	13.30	4.47	1.87
Vermont	312	652	99	303	1505	−.784	2.700	3.326	3.19	.158	23.80	2.14	
Virginia	366	283	128		1411	−.447	2.349	3.365		.171	13.92	2.49	.38
Washington	515	316	345	130	1809	−.730	2.495	3.507	3.17	.464	12.40	3.67	
West Virginia	333	206	83		1304	−.249	1.986	3.367		.117	9.28	1.93	.10
Wisconsin	513	456	337	6	1641	−.358	2.206	3.745	2.65	.295	17.34	3.79	
Wyoming	661	355	184		1789	−.439	2.496	3.453		.165	16.77	3.11	

Bibliography

1. Alhadeff, D. A., "Credit Controls and Financial Intermediaries," *Am. Econ. Rev.*, Sept., 1960, **50,** 655–71.

2. Aschheim, J., "Commercial Bank and Financial Intermediaries: Fallacies and Policy Implications," *Jour. Pol. Econ.*, Feb., 1959, **67,** 59–71.

3. Baumol, W. J., "Pitfalls in Contracyclical Policies: Some Tools and Results," *Rev. Econ. Stat.*, Feb., 1961, **43,** 21–26.

4. Bronfenbrenner, M., and T. Mayer, "Liquidity Functions in the American Economy," *Econometrica*, Oct., 1960, **28,** 810–34.

5. Cagan, P., "The Demand for Currency Relative to the Total Money Supply," *Jour. Pol. Econ.*, Aug., 1958, **66,** 303–28.

6. ———, "Why Do We Use Money in Open Market Operations?" *Jour. Pol. Econ.*, Feb., 1958, **66,** 34–46.

7. Christ, C. F., "Interest Rates and 'Portfolio Selection' among Liquid Assets in the U.S.," *Measurement in Economics: Studies in Mathematical Economics and Econometrics in Memory of Yehuda Grunfeld.* Stanford, Calif.: Stanford University Press, 1963, pp. 201–218.

8. Culbertson, J. M., "Intermediaries and Monetary Theory: A Criticism of the Gurley-Shaw Theory," *Am. Econ. Rev.*, Mar., 1958, **48,** 119–31.

9. Durbin, J., and G. S. Watson, "Testing for Serial Correlation in Least Squares Regression," *Biometrika*, 1951, **38,** 159–78.

10. Friedman, M., *A Theory of the Consumption Function.* Princeton, 1957.

11. ———, "The Demand for Money," *Am. Phil. Soc. Proc.*, June, 1961, **105,** 259–64.

12. ———, "The Demand for Money: Some Theoretical and Empirical Results," *Jour. Pol. Econ.*, Aug., 1959, **67,** 327–51.

13. ———, "The Quantity Theory of Money—A Restatement," in M. Friedman, ed., *Studies in the Quantity Theory of Money*. Chicago, 1956, pp. 3–21.

14. ———, and D. Meiselman, *The Relative Stability of Monetary Velocity and the Investment Multiplier in the United States, 1897–1958*. (Forthcoming publication of the Commission on Money and Credit.)

15. Goldsmith, R. W., *Financial Intermediaries in the American Economy Since 1900*. Princeton, 1958.

16. Gurley, J. G., *Liquidity and Financial Institutions in the Postwar Economy*. Study Paper 14, Joint Economic Committee, 86th Cong., 2nd Sess., Washington, 1960.

17. ———, and E. S. Shaw, "Financial Aspects of Economic Development," *Am. Econ. Rev.*, Sept., 1955, **45,** 515–38.

18. ———, and ———, "Financial Intermediaries and the Saving-Investment Process," *Jour. Finance*, May, 1956, **11,** 257–76.

19. ———, and ———, *Money in a Theory of Finance*. Washington, D.C.: Brookings Institution, 1960.

20. ———, and ———, "The Growth of Debt, and Money in the United States, 1800–1950: A Suggested Interpretation," *Rev. Econ. Stat.*, Aug., 1957, **39,** 250–62.

21. Hicks, J. R., "A Suggestion for Simplifying the Theory of Money," *Economica*, Feb., 1935, **2,** 1–19; reprinted in F. A. Lutz and L. W. Mints, eds., *Readings in Monetary Theory*. Homewood, Ill., 1951, pp. 13–32.

22. Johnson, H. G., "Monetary Theory and Policy," *Am. Econ. Rev.*, June, 1962, **52,** 335–84.

23. Kullback, S., and H. M. Rosenblatt, "On the Analysis of Multiple Regression in K Categories," *Biometrika*, 1957, **44,** 67–83.

24. Latané, H. A., "Cash Balances and the Interest Rate—A Pragmatic Approach," *Rev. Econ. Stat.*, Nov., 1954, **36,** 456–60.

25. ———, "Income Velocity and Interest Rates—A Pragmatic Approach," *Rev. Econ. Stat.*, Nov., 1960, **42,** 445–49.

26. Lydall, H. F., "Income, Assets and the Demand for Money," *Rev. Econ. Stat.*, Feb., 1958, **40,** 1–14.

27. Markowitz, H. M., *Portfolio Selection: Efficient Diversification of Investments.* New York, 1959.

28. Marty, A. L., "Gurley and Shaw on Money in a Theory of Finance," *Jour. Pol. Econ.*, Feb., 1961, **69,** 56–62.

29. McKean, R. N., "Liquidity and a National Balance Sheet," *Jour. Pol. Econ.*, Dec., 1949, **57,** 506–22; reprinted in F. A. Lutz and L. W. Mints, eds., *Readings in Monetary Theory.* Homewood, Ill., 1951, pp. 63–88.

30. Patinkin, D., "Financial Intermediaries and the Logical Structure of Monetary Theory," *Am. Econ. Rev.*, Mar., 1961, **51,** 95–116.

31. ———, *Money, Interest and Prices.* Evanston, Ill., 1956.

32. Prais, S., and H. Houthakker, *The Analysis of Family Budgets.* Cambridge, 1955.

33. Rousseas, S. W., "Velocity Changes and the Effectiveness of Monetary Policy, 1951–57," *Rev. Econ. Stat.*, Feb., 1960, **42,** 27–36.

34. Roy, S. W., *Some Aspects of Multivariate Analysis.* New York, 1957.

35. Schultz, H., *The Theory and Measurement of Demand.* Chicago, 1938.

36. Selden, R. T., "Monetary Velocity in the United States," in Milton Friedman, ed., *Studies in the Quantity Theory of Money.* Chicago, 1956, pp. 179–257.

37. Shelby, D., "Some Implications of the Growth of Financial Intermediaries," *Jour. Finance*, Dec., 1958, **13,** 527–41.

38. Smith, W. L., "Financial Intermediaries and Monetary Controls," *Quart. Jour. Econ.*, Nov., 1959, **73,** 533–53.

39. ———, "On the Effectiveness of Monetary Policy," *Am. Econ. Rev.*, Sept., 1956, **46,** 588–606.

40. Theil, H., *Economic Forecasts and Policy.* Amsterdam, 1958.

41. ———, and A. S. Goldberger, "On Pure and Mixed Statistical Estimation in Economics," *Internatl. Econ. Rev.*, 1960, 2.

42. Tobin, J., "Liquidity Preference and Monetary Policy," *Rev. Econ. Stat.*, May, 1947, **29,** 124–31.

43. ———, "Money, Capital and Other Stores of Value," *Am. Econ. Rev. Proc.*, May, 1961, **51,** 26–37.

44. Tobin, J., "Monetary Theory: New and Old Looks," *Am. Econ. Rev.*, May, 1961, **51,** 26–37.

45. ———, "The Interest-Elasticity of Transactions Demand for Cash," *Rev. Econ. Stat.*, Aug., 1956, **38,** 241–47.

46. ———, and W. C. Brainard, "Financial Intermediaries and the Effectiveness of Monetary Controls." Unpublished paper delivered at the meetings of the Econometric Society, December, 1962.

47. Tsiang, S. C., "Liquidity Preference and Loanable Funds Theories, Multiplier and Velocity Analysis: A Synthesis," *Am. Econ. Rev.*, Sept., 1956, **46,** 539–64.

48. Wold, H., *Demand Analysis.* New York, 1953.

49. Zellner, A., "An Efficient Method of Estimating Seemingly Unrelated Regressions and Tests for Aggregation Bias," *Jour. Am. Stat. Assoc.*, June, 1962, **57,** 348–68.

SOURCES OF DATA

1. Comptroller of the Currency, *Annual Reports*, 1949–1959.

2. Federal Deposit Insurance Corporation, *Annual Reports*, 1949–1959.

3. Federal Home Loan Bank Board, *Combined Financial Statements*, 1949–1959.

4. U.S. Department of Commerce, *Personal Income by States since 1929: A Supplement to the Survey of Current Business*, 1956.

5. United States Savings and Loan League, *Annual Statistical Reports*, 1949–1959.

DATE DUE